7-13

Lost Trail

Nine Days Alone in the
Wilderness

D0730853

Lost Trail

Nine Days Alone in the Wilderness

by **Donn Fendler**
with **Lynn Plourde**   illustrated by **Ben Bishop**

Down East Books

MONTROSE REGIONAL LIBRARY
320 SO. 2ND ST.
MONTROSE, CO 81401

Text Copyright © 2011 Donn Fendler and Lynn Plourde
Illustration Copyright © 2011 Benjamin Bishop

Printed in the United States

Distributed to the trade
by National Book Network

ISBN: 978-0-89272-945-6

DownEastBooks
www.nbnbooks.com

The newspaper clippings in this book are depicted to be from the Bangor Daily
News, *which had the most comprehensive coverage of Donn Fendler's 1939 saga
and provided AP reports to the rest of the country. But the accounts themselves are
actually fictional versions based upon combined information obtained from Donn
Fendler and his family, and details on the search efforts from the* Bangor Daily
News *and the book,* Lost on a Mountain in Maine, *by Joseph B. Egan.*

To Ree, who gave all of herself to our family.
Truly missed
—DF

For Donn, a true friend
and a true hero
—LP

To Meagan and the dogs,
family and friends, Donn for his story,
and Ari for the opportunity
—RR

IT'S HARD TO BELIEVE MORE THAN SEVENTY YEARS HAVE PASSED SINCE I GAVE DEATH A LONG, HARD STARE. THERE'S NO WAY I SHOULD HAVE SURVIVED THAT 1939 RUN-IN WITH MOUNT KATAHDIN, THOSE NINE DAYS ALONE IN THE MAINE WILDERNESS. BUT I DID. I LIVED MY OWN PERSONAL MIRACLE WHEN I WAS ONLY TWELVE YEARS OLD.

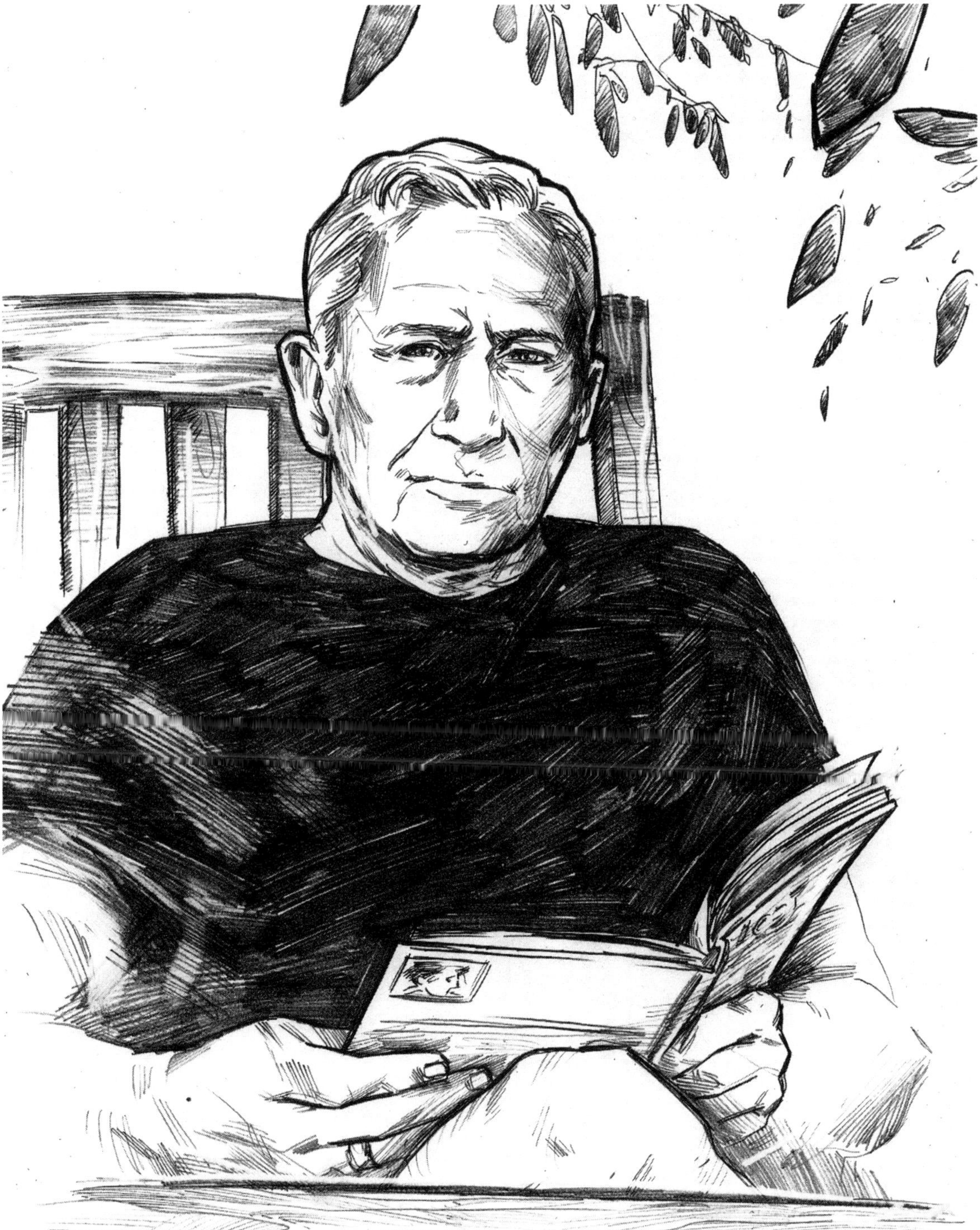

WHENEVER I LOOK IN THE MIRROR, IT'S OBVIOUS DECADES HAVE PASSED. BUT AT THE SAME TIME, MY ORDEAL SEEMS SO REAL, LIKE YESTERDAY. I SCRATCH AT THE THOUGHT OF THE BUGS' RELENTLESS BLOODY GNAWING. THE MEMORY OF THE BEAR'S STEELY STARE MAKES ME FLINCH. AND THE ACHE, THE AWFUL ACHE OF THE FEAR AND THE LONELINESS ARE STILL HAUNTINGLY REAL.

I NEVER SHOULD HAVE CLIMBED KATAHDIN IN THE FIRST PLACE. WE HAD OTHER PLANS...

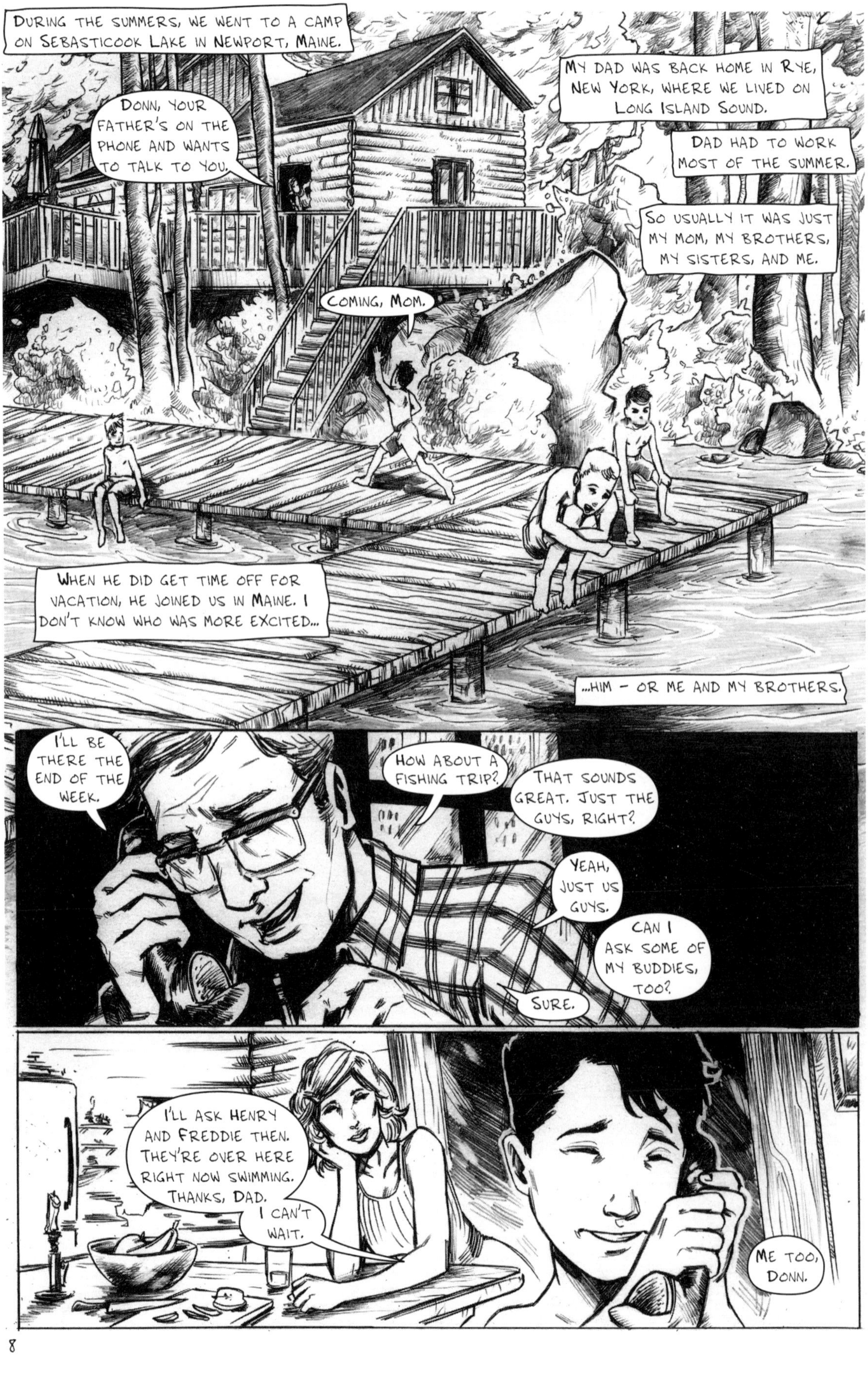
During the summers, we went to a camp on Sebasticook Lake in Newport, Maine.
Donn, your father's on the phone and wants to talk to you.
My dad was back home in Rye, New York, where we lived on Long Island Sound.
Dad had to work most of the summer.
So usually it was just my mom, my brothers, my sisters, and me.
Coming, Mom.
When he did get time off for vacation, he joined us in Maine. I don't know who was more excited...
...him - or me and my brothers.
I'll be there the end of the week.
How about a fishing trip?
That sounds great. Just the guys, right?
Yeah, just us guys.
Can I ask some of my buddies, too?
Sure.
I'll ask Henry and Freddie then. They're over here right now swimming. Thanks, Dad.
I can't wait.
Me too, Donn.

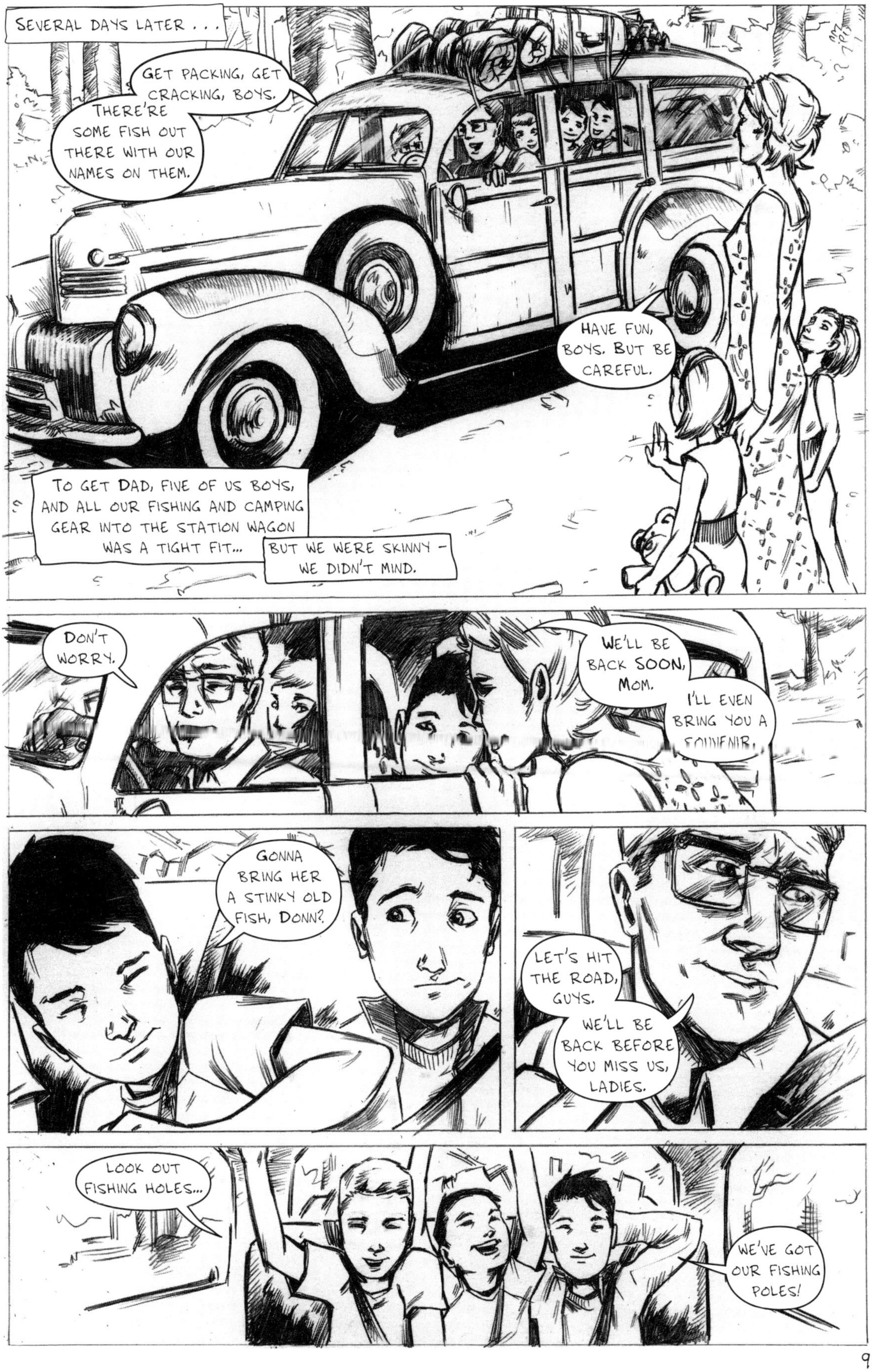
SEVERAL DAYS LATER . . .
GET PACKING, GET CRACKING, BOYS.
THERE'RE SOME FISH OUT THERE WITH OUR NAMES ON THEM.
HAVE FUN, BOYS. BUT BE CAREFUL.
TO GET DAD, FIVE OF US BOYS, AND ALL OUR FISHING AND CAMPING GEAR INTO THE STATION WAGON WAS A TIGHT FIT...
BUT WE WERE SKINNY – WE DIDN'T MIND.
DON'T WORRY.
WE'LL BE BACK SOON, MOM.
I'LL EVEN BRING YOU A SOUVENIR.
GONNA BRING HER A STINKY OLD FISH, DONN?
LET'S HIT THE ROAD, GUYS.
WE'LL BE BACK BEFORE YOU MISS US, LADIES.
LOOK OUT FISHING HOLES...
WE'VE GOT OUR FISHING POLES!

Our plan was to travel north as far as Caribou in Aroostook County in northern Maine and hit as many fishing spots as we could along the way. Our first stop was Milo, where we set up camp along the Sebec River. We only caught a few brookies, but we didn't mind.

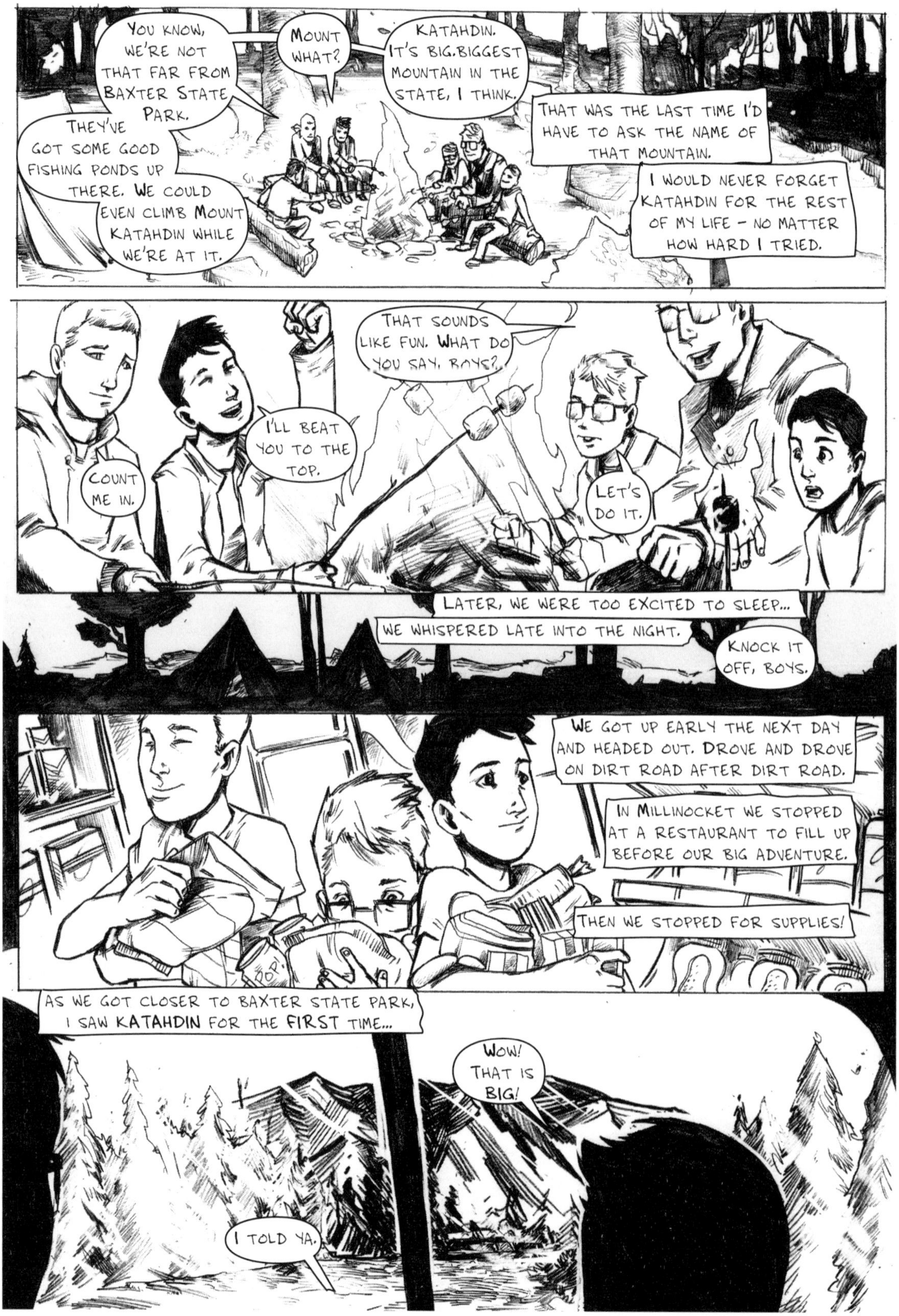
You know, we're not that far from Baxter State Park.
They've got some good fishing ponds up there. We could even climb Mount Katahdin while we're at it.
Mount what?
Katahdin. It's big. Biggest mountain in the state, I think.
That was the last time I'd have to ask the name of that mountain.
I would never forget Katahdin for the rest of my life – no matter how hard I tried.
That sounds like fun. What do you say, boys?
Count me in.
I'll beat you to the top.
Let's do it.
Later, we were too excited to sleep...
We whispered late into the night.
Knock it off, boys.
We got up early the next day and headed out. Drove and drove on dirt road after dirt road.
In Millinocket we stopped at a restaurant to fill up before our big adventure.
Then we stopped for supplies!
As we got closer to Baxter State Park, I saw Katahdin for the first time...
Wow! That is big!
I told ya.

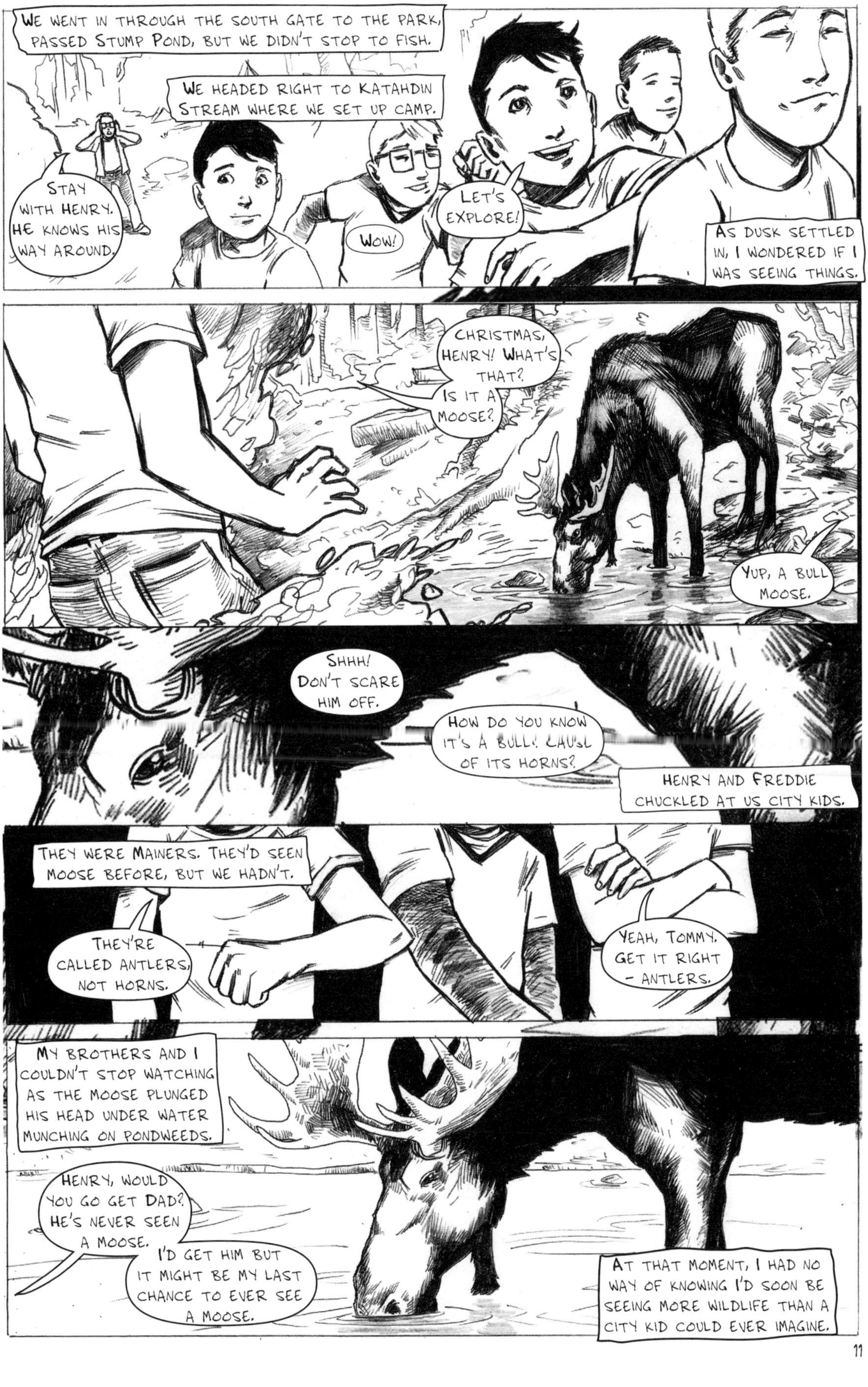

We went in through the south gate to the park, passed Stump Pond, but we didn't stop to fish.
We headed right to Katahdin Stream where we set up camp.
Stay with Henry. He knows his way around.
Wow!
Let's explore!
As dusk settled in, I wondered if I was seeing things.
Christmas, Henry! What's that?
Is it a moose?
Yup, a bull moose.
Shhh! Don't scare him off.
How do you know it's a bull? Cause of its horns?
Henry and Freddie chuckled at us city kids.
They were Mainers. They'd seen moose before, but we hadn't.
They're called antlers, not horns.
Yeah, Tommy. Get it right - antlers.
My brothers and I couldn't stop watching as the moose plunged his head under water munching on pondweeds.
Henry, would you go get Dad? He's never seen a moose.
I'd get him but it might be my last chance to ever see a moose.
At that moment, I had no way of knowing I'd soon be seeing more wildlife than a city kid could ever imagine.

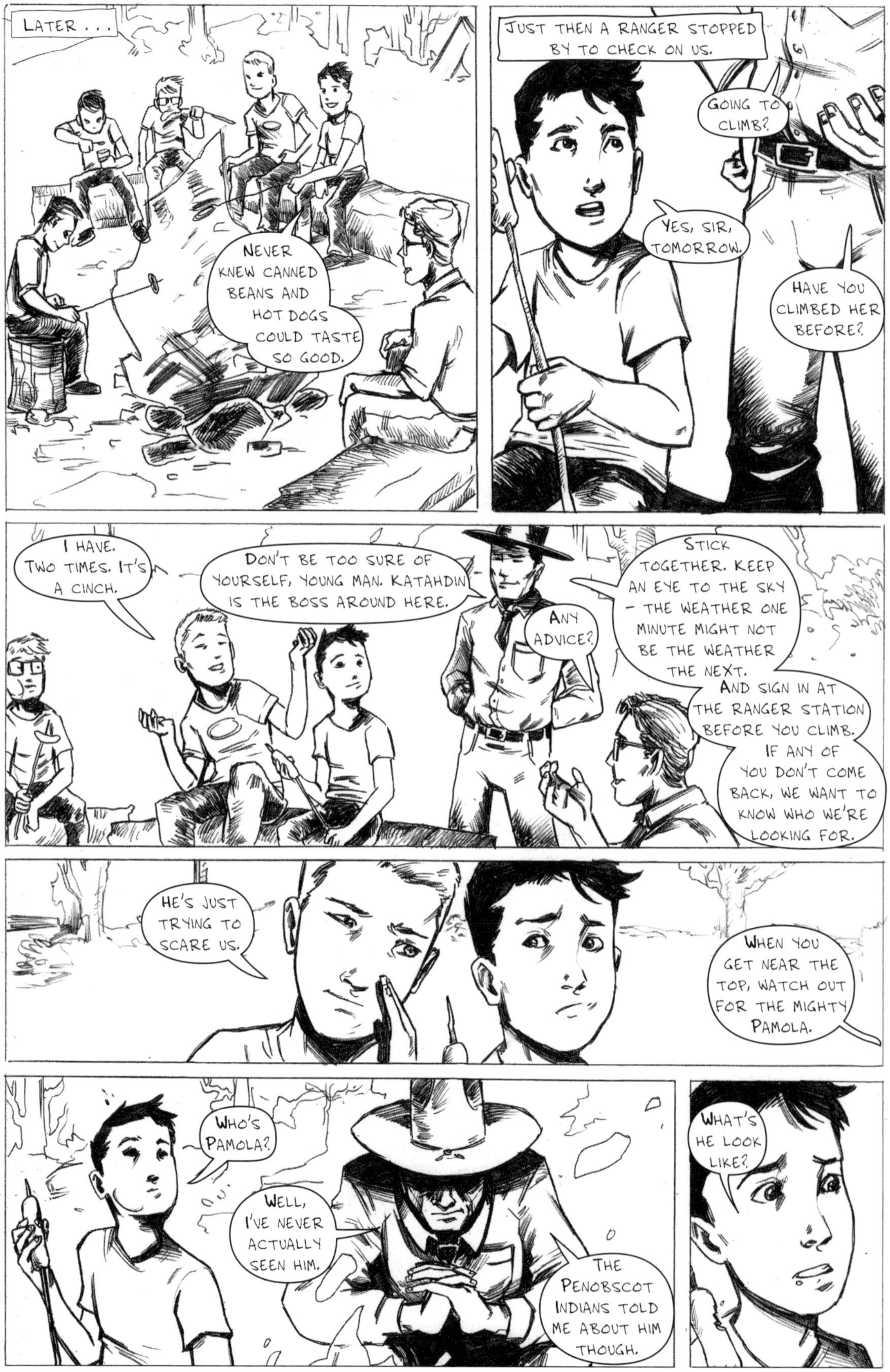

LATER . . .
NEVER KNEW CANNED BEANS AND HOT DOGS COULD TASTE SO GOOD.
JUST THEN A RANGER STOPPED BY TO CHECK ON US.
GOING TO CLIMB?
YES, SIR, TOMORROW.
HAVE YOU CLIMBED HER BEFORE?
I HAVE. TWO TIMES. IT'S A CINCH.
DON'T BE TOO SURE OF YOURSELF, YOUNG MAN. KATAHDIN IS THE BOSS AROUND HERE.
ANY ADVICE?
STICK TOGETHER. KEEP AN EYE TO THE SKY - THE WEATHER ONE MINUTE MIGHT NOT BE THE WEATHER THE NEXT.
AND SIGN IN AT THE RANGER STATION BEFORE YOU CLIMB.
IF ANY OF YOU DON'T COME BACK, WE WANT TO KNOW WHO WE'RE LOOKING FOR.
HE'S JUST TRYING TO SCARE US.
WHEN YOU GET NEAR THE TOP, WATCH OUT FOR THE MIGHTY PAMOLA.
WHO'S PAMOLA?
WELL, I'VE NEVER ACTUALLY SEEN HIM.
THE PENOBSCOT INDIANS TOLD ME ABOUT HIM THOUGH.
WHAT'S HE LOOK LIKE?

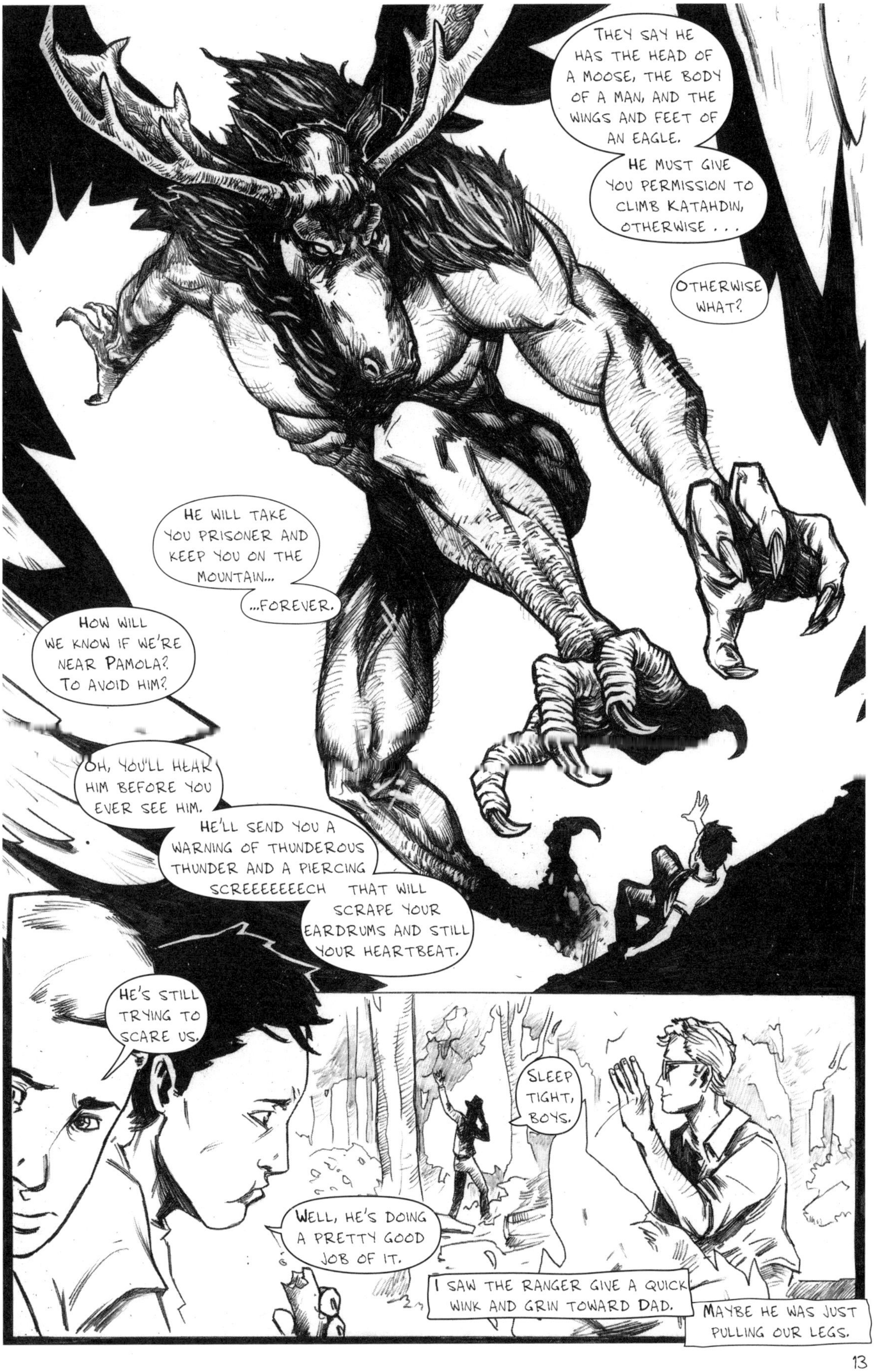
THEY SAY HE HAS THE HEAD OF A MOOSE, THE BODY OF A MAN, AND THE WINGS AND FEET OF AN EAGLE.
HE MUST GIVE YOU PERMISSION TO CLIMB KATAHDIN, OTHERWISE . . .
OTHERWISE WHAT?
HE WILL TAKE YOU PRISONER AND KEEP YOU ON THE MOUNTAIN...
...FOREVER.
HOW WILL WE KNOW IF WE'RE NEAR PAMOLA? TO AVOID HIM?
OH, YOU'LL HEAR HIM BEFORE YOU EVER SEE HIM.
HE'LL SEND YOU A WARNING OF THUNDEROUS THUNDER AND A PIERCING SCREEEEEEECH THAT WILL SCRAPE YOUR EARDRUMS AND STILL YOUR HEARTBEAT.
HE'S STILL TRYING TO SCARE US.
SLEEP TIGHT, BOYS.
WELL, HE'S DOING A PRETTY GOOD JOB OF IT.
I SAW THE RANGER GIVE A QUICK WINK AND GRIN TOWARD DAD.
MAYBE HE WAS JUST PULLING OUR LEGS.

DAY ONE

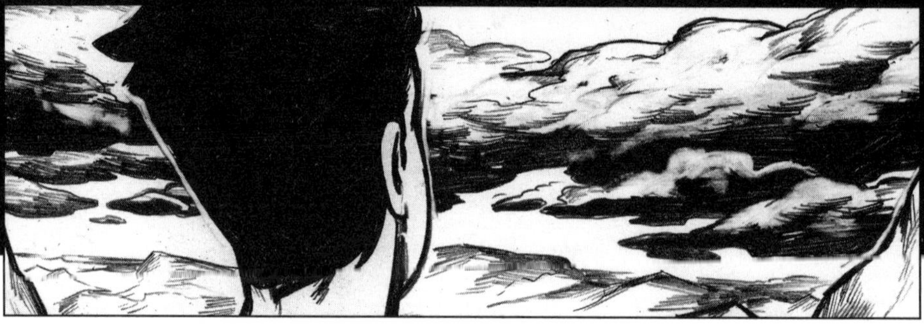

In the morning, after a breakfast of bacon, leftover beans, and bread-on-a-stick, we broke down camp.

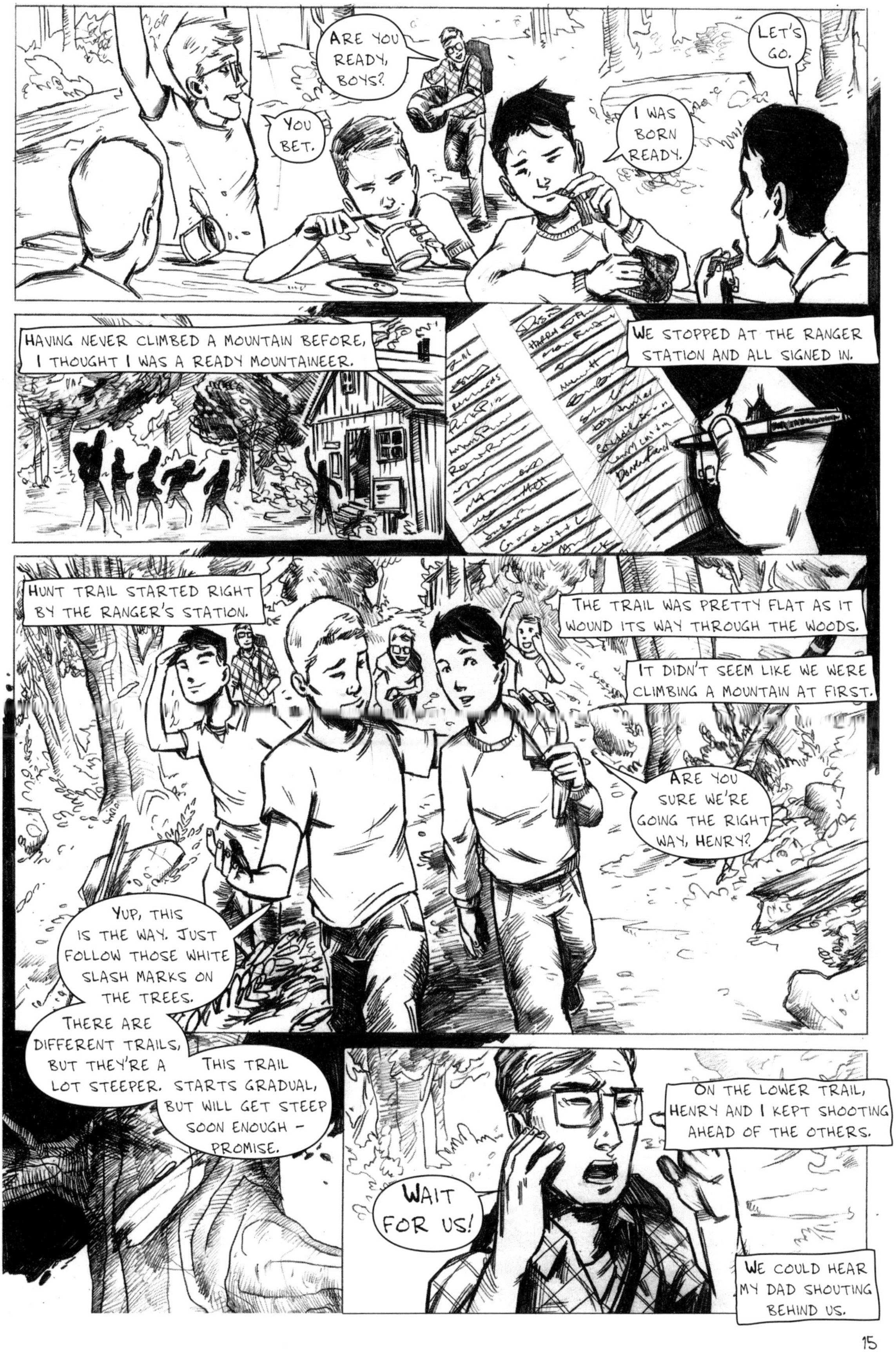

Are you ready, boys?
You bet.
I was born ready.
Let's go.
Having never climbed a mountain before, I thought I was a ready mountaineer.
We stopped at the ranger station and all signed in.
Hunt trail started right by the ranger's station.
The trail was pretty flat as it wound its way through the woods.
It didn't seem like we were climbing a mountain at first.
Are you sure we're going the right way, Henry?
Yup, this is the way. Just follow those white slash marks on the trees.
There are different trails, but they're a lot steeper.
This trail starts gradual, but will get steep soon enough - promise.
On the lower trail, Henry and I kept shooting ahead of the others.
Wait for us!
We could hear my dad shouting behind us.

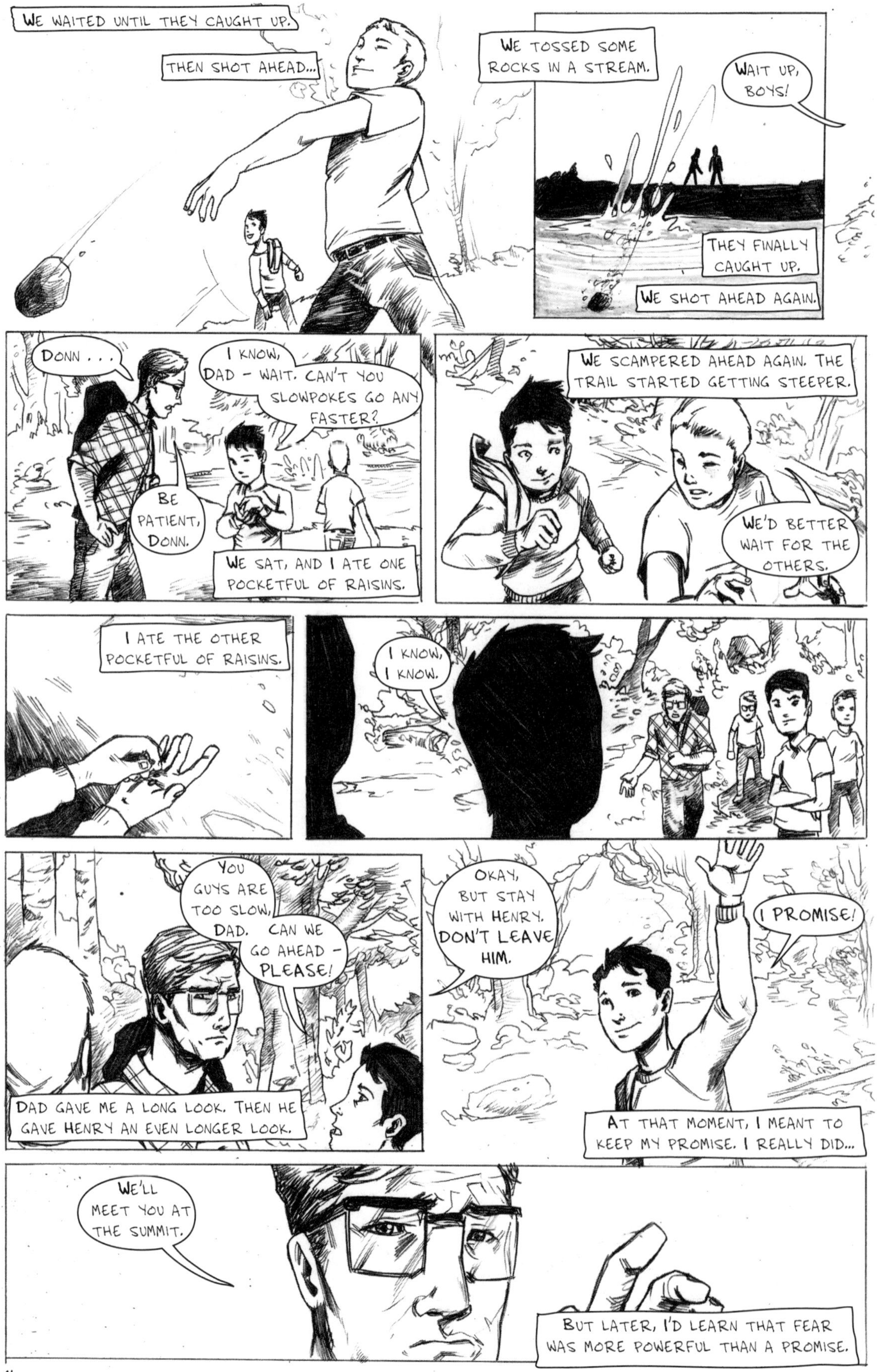
We waited until they caught up.
Then shot ahead...
We tossed some rocks in a stream.
Wait up, boys!
They finally caught up.
We shot ahead again.
Donn . . .
I know, Dad - wait. Can't you slowpokes go any faster?
Be patient, Donn.
We sat, and I ate one pocketful of raisins.
We scampered ahead again. The trail started getting steeper.
We'd better wait for the others.
I ate the other pocketful of raisins.
I know, I know.
You guys are too slow, Dad. Can we go ahead - PLEASE!
Dad gave me a long look. Then he gave Henry an even longer look.
Okay, but stay with Henry. DON'T LEAVE HIM.
I PROMISE!
At that moment, I meant to keep my promise. I really did...
We'll meet you at the summit.
But later, I'd learn that fear was more powerful than a promise.

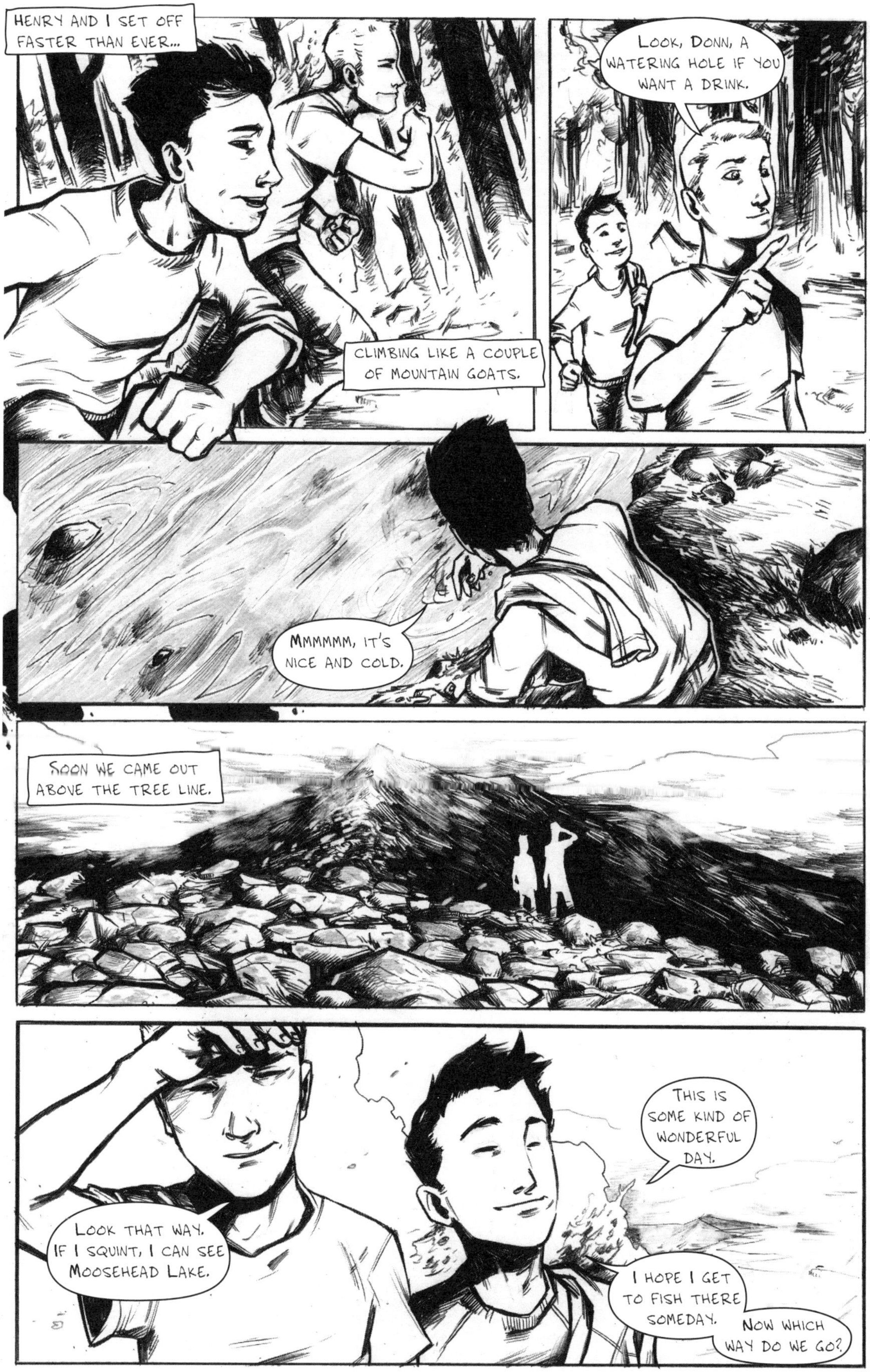
HENRY AND I SET OFF FASTER THAN EVER...
CLIMBING LIKE A COUPLE OF MOUNTAIN GOATS.
LOOK, DONN, A WATERING HOLE IF YOU WANT A DRINK.
MMMMMM, IT'S NICE AND COLD.
SOON WE CAME OUT ABOVE THE TREE LINE.
THIS IS SOME KIND OF WONDERFUL DAY.
LOOK THAT WAY. IF I SQUINT, I CAN SEE MOOSEHEAD LAKE.
I HOPE I GET TO FISH THERE SOMEDAY.
NOW WHICH WAY DO WE GO?

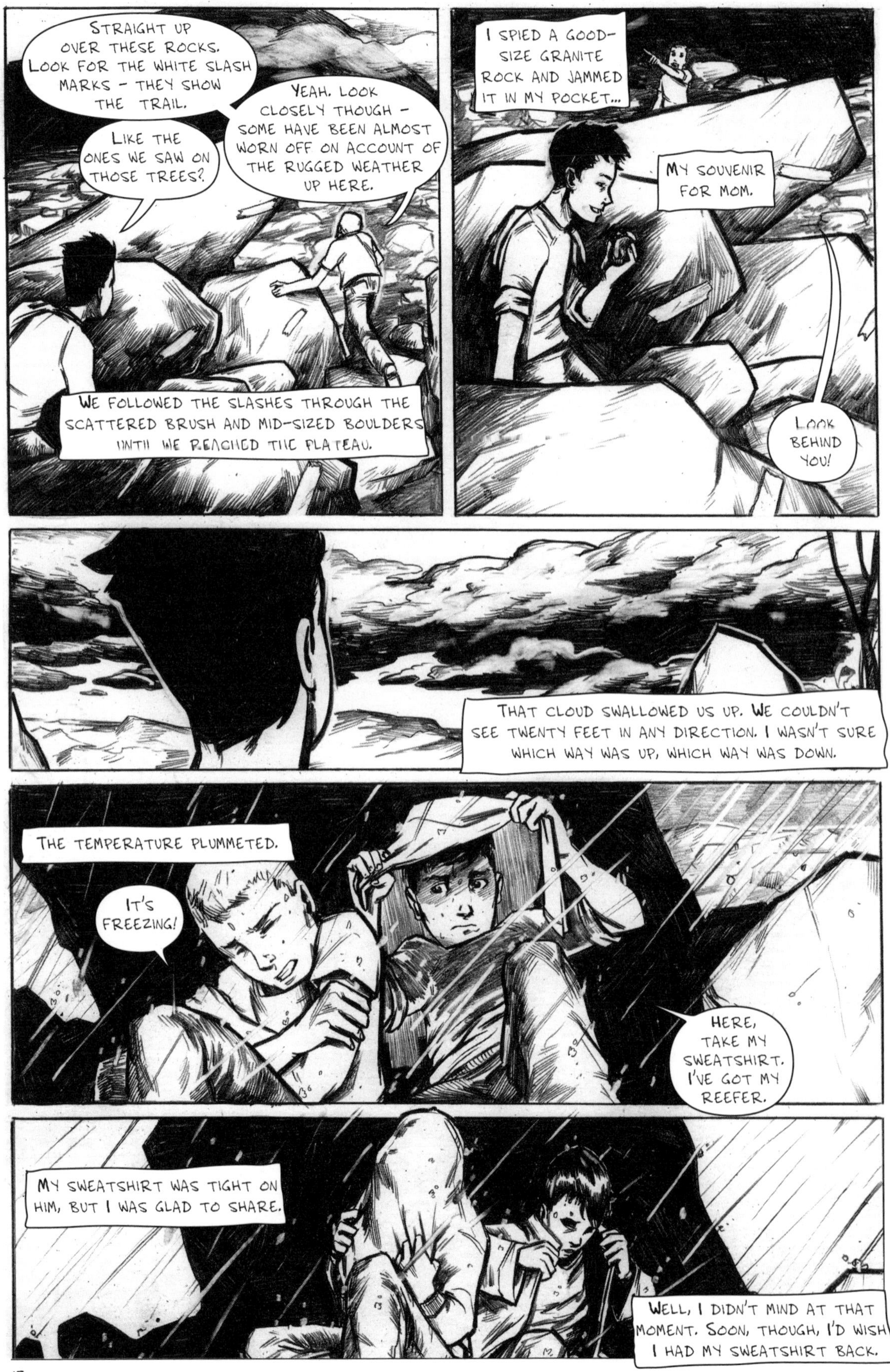
Straight up over these rocks. Look for the white slash marks - they show the trail.
Like the ones we saw on those trees?
Yeah. Look closely though - some have been almost worn off on account of the rugged weather up here.
We followed the slashes through the scattered brush and mid-sized boulders until we reached the plateau.
I spied a good-size granite rock and jammed it in my pocket...
My souvenir for Mom.
Look behind you!
That cloud swallowed us up. We couldn't see twenty feet in any direction. I wasn't sure which way was up, which way was down.
The temperature plummeted.
It's freezing!
Here, take my sweatshirt. I've got my reefer.
My sweatshirt was tight on him, but I was glad to share.
Well, I didn't mind at that moment. Soon, though, I'd wish I had my sweatshirt back.

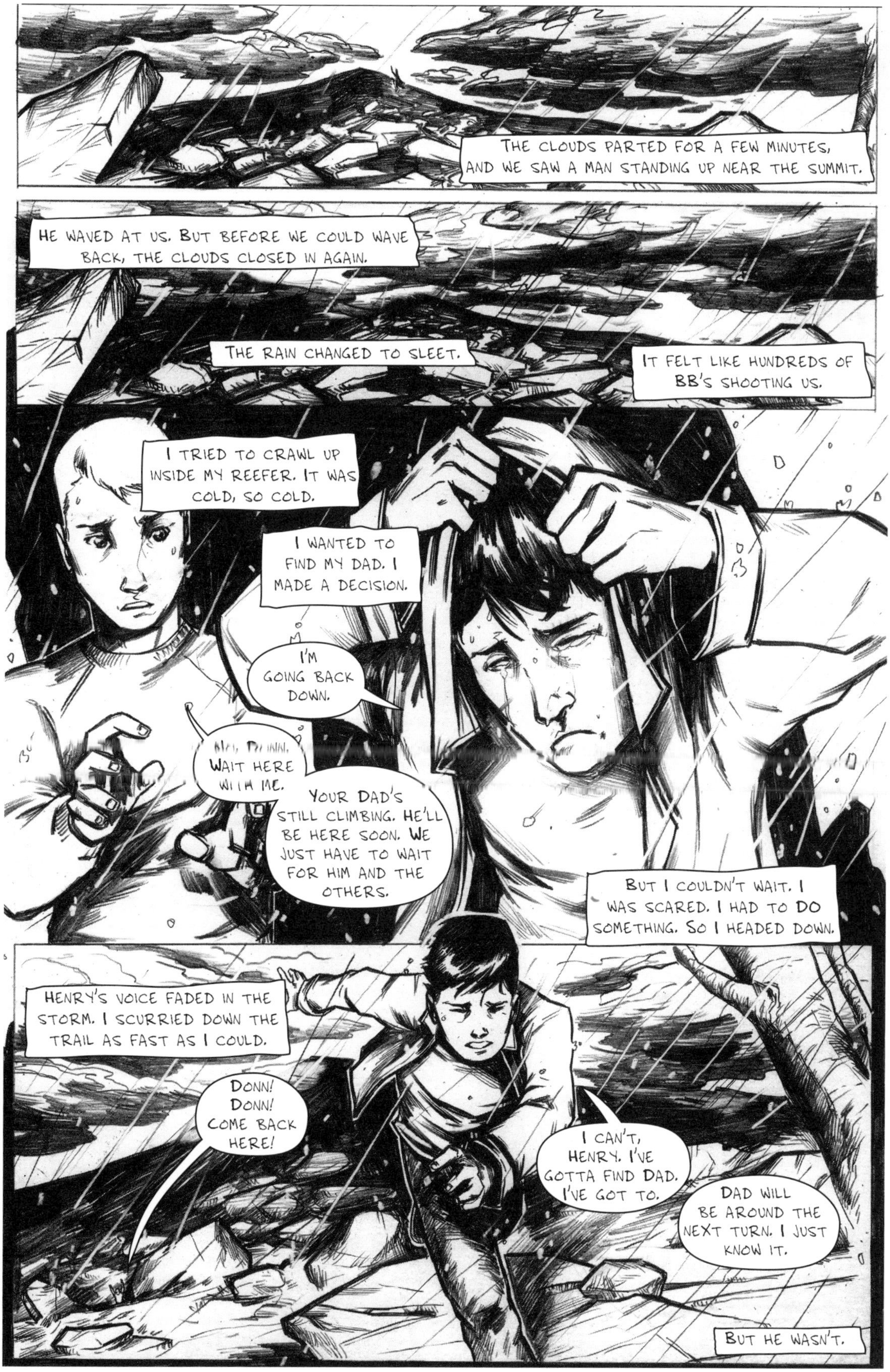
THE CLOUDS PARTED FOR A FEW MINUTES, AND WE SAW A MAN STANDING UP NEAR THE SUMMIT.
HE WAVED AT US. BUT BEFORE WE COULD WAVE BACK, THE CLOUDS CLOSED IN AGAIN.
THE RAIN CHANGED TO SLEET.
IT FELT LIKE HUNDREDS OF BB'S SHOOTING US.
I TRIED TO CRAWL UP INSIDE MY REEFER. IT WAS COLD, SO COLD.
I WANTED TO FIND MY DAD. I MADE A DECISION.
I'M GOING BACK DOWN.
WAIT HERE WITH ME.
YOUR DAD'S STILL CLIMBING. HE'LL BE HERE SOON. WE JUST HAVE TO WAIT FOR HIM AND THE OTHERS.
BUT I COULDN'T WAIT. I WAS SCARED. I HAD TO DO SOMETHING. SO I HEADED DOWN.
HENRY'S VOICE FADED IN THE STORM. I SCURRIED DOWN THE TRAIL AS FAST AS I COULD.
DONN! DONN! COME BACK HERE!
I CAN'T, HENRY. I'VE GOTTA FIND DAD. I'VE GOT TO.
DAD WILL BE AROUND THE NEXT TURN. I JUST KNOW IT.
BUT HE WASN'T.

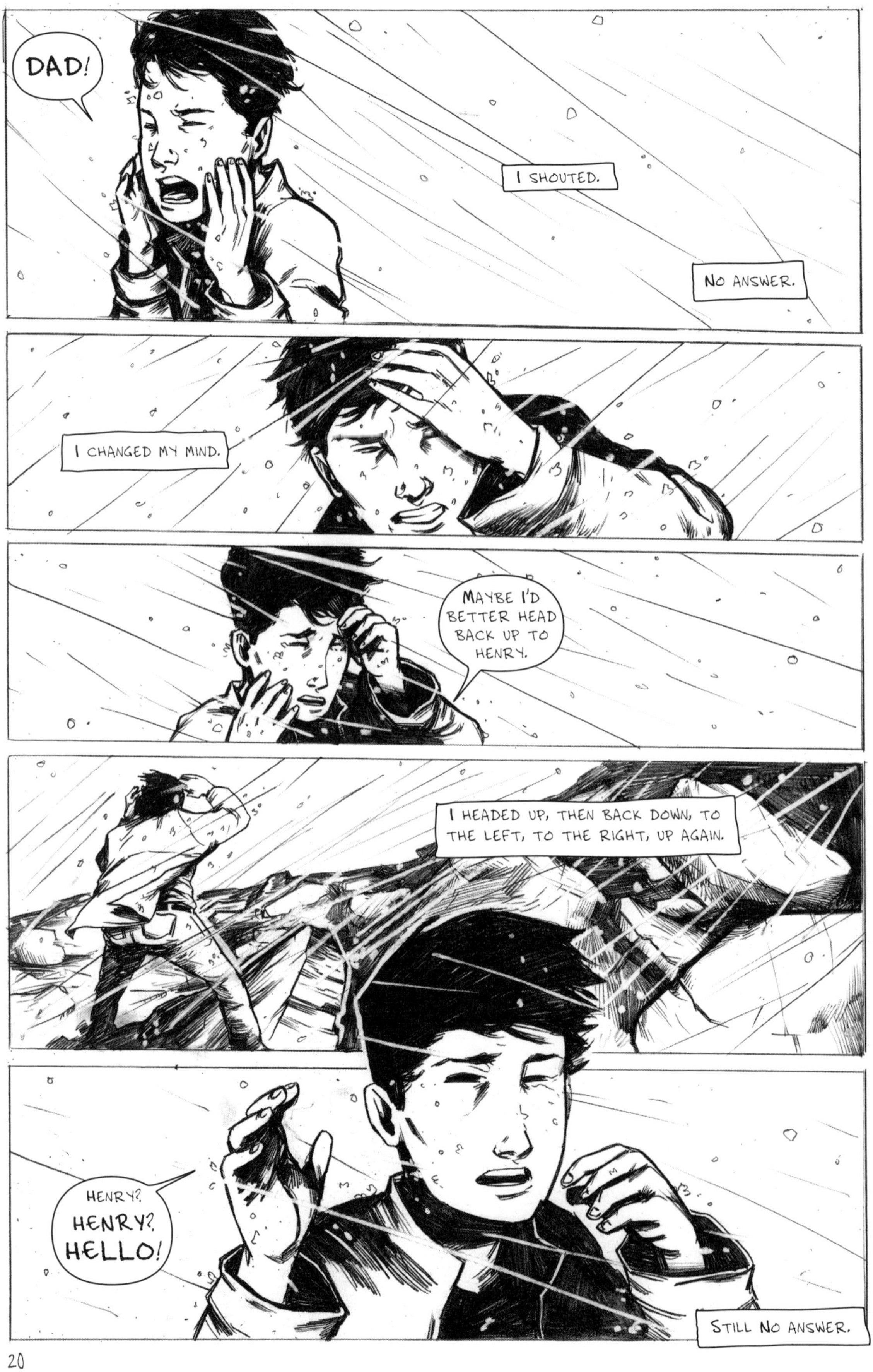
DAD!
I SHOUTED.
NO ANSWER.
I CHANGED MY MIND.
MAYBE I'D BETTER HEAD BACK UP TO HENRY.
I HEADED UP, THEN BACK DOWN, TO THE LEFT, TO THE RIGHT, UP AGAIN.
HENRY? HENRY? HELLO!
STILL NO ANSWER.

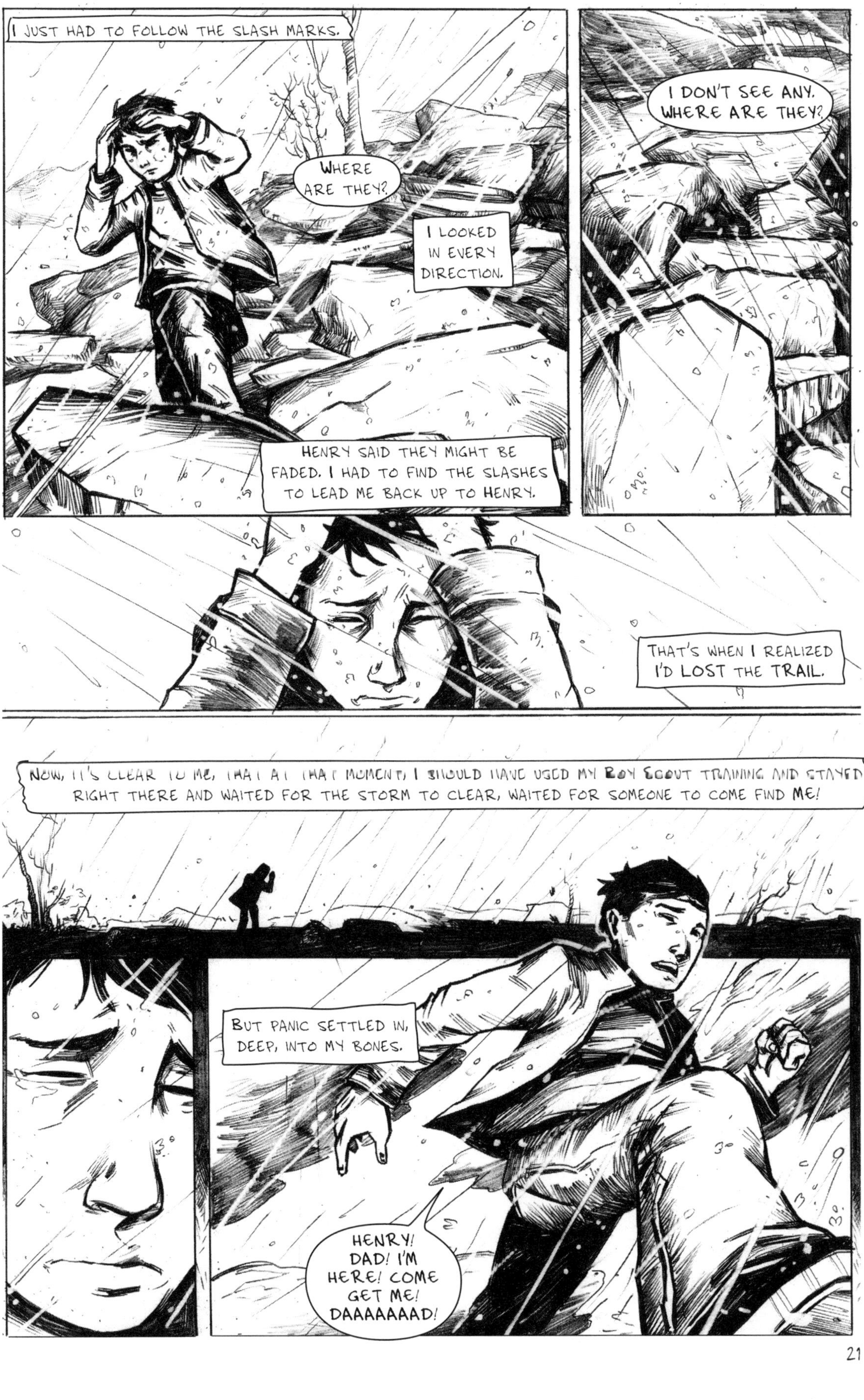
I JUST HAD TO FOLLOW THE SLASH MARKS.
WHERE ARE THEY?
I LOOKED IN EVERY DIRECTION.
I DON'T SEE ANY. WHERE ARE THEY?
HENRY SAID THEY MIGHT BE FADED. I HAD TO FIND THE SLASHES TO LEAD ME BACK UP TO HENRY.
THAT'S WHEN I REALIZED I'D LOST THE TRAIL.
NOW, IT'S CLEAR TO ME, THAT AT THAT MOMENT, I SHOULD HAVE USED MY BOY SCOUT TRAINING AND STAYED RIGHT THERE AND WAITED FOR THE STORM TO CLEAR, WAITED FOR SOMEONE TO COME FIND ME!
BUT PANIC SETTLED IN, DEEP, INTO MY BONES.
HENRY! DAD! I'M HERE! COME GET ME! DAAAAAAAD!

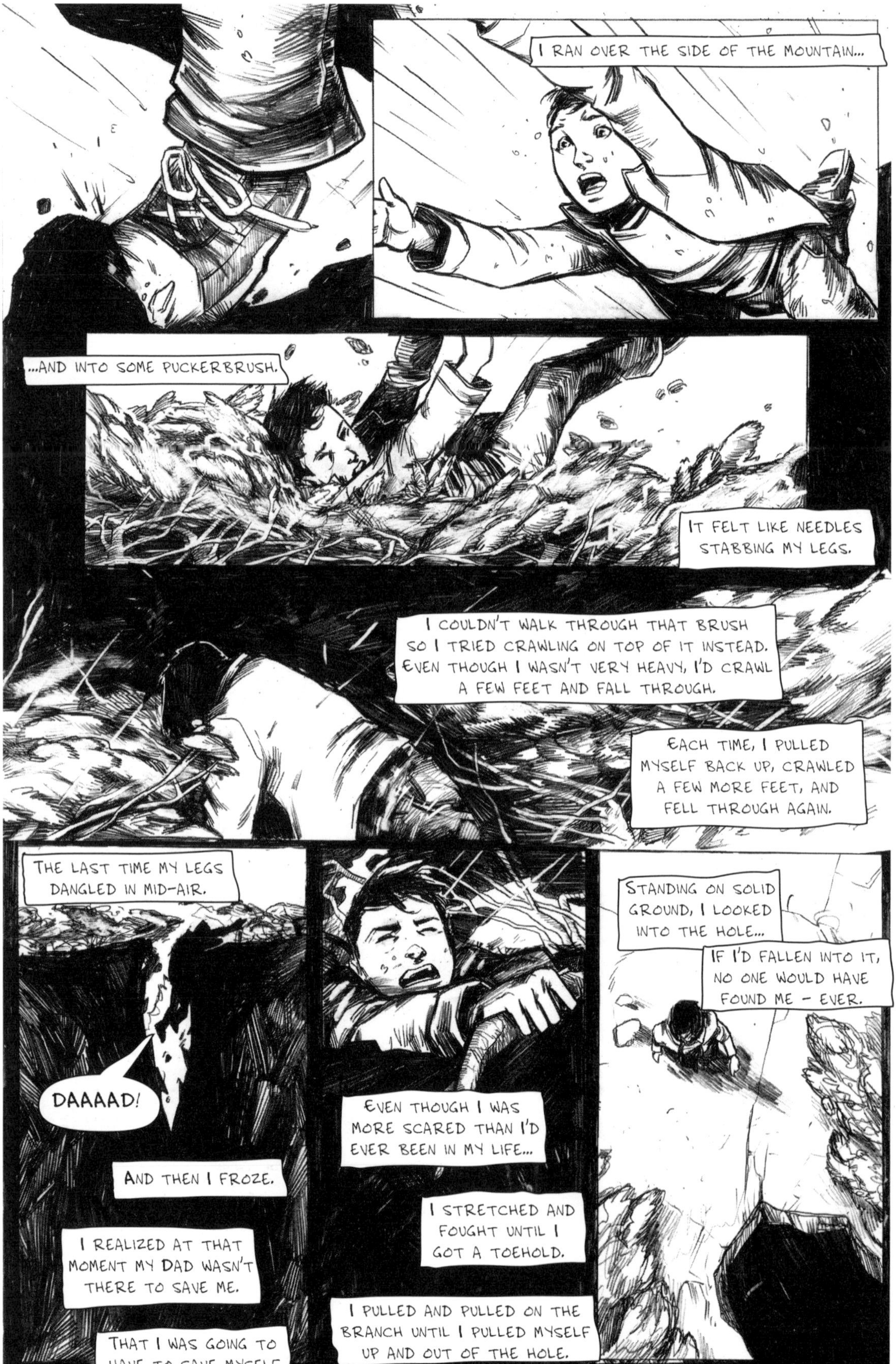
I RAN OVER THE SIDE OF THE MOUNTAIN...
...AND INTO SOME PUCKERBRUSH.
IT FELT LIKE NEEDLES STABBING MY LEGS.
I COULDN'T WALK THROUGH THAT BRUSH SO I TRIED CRAWLING ON TOP OF IT INSTEAD. EVEN THOUGH I WASN'T VERY HEAVY, I'D CRAWL A FEW FEET AND FALL THROUGH.
EACH TIME, I PULLED MYSELF BACK UP, CRAWLED A FEW MORE FEET, AND FELL THROUGH AGAIN.
THE LAST TIME MY LEGS DANGLED IN MID-AIR.
DAAAAD!
AND THEN I FROZE.
I REALIZED AT THAT MOMENT MY DAD WASN'T THERE TO SAVE ME.
THAT I WAS GOING TO HAVE TO SAVE MYSELF.
EVEN THOUGH I WAS MORE SCARED THAN I'D EVER BEEN IN MY LIFE...
I STRETCHED AND FOUGHT UNTIL I GOT A TOEHOLD.
I PULLED AND PULLED ON THE BRANCH UNTIL I PULLED MYSELF UP AND OUT OF THE HOLE.
STANDING ON SOLID GROUND, I LOOKED INTO THE HOLE...
IF I'D FALLEN INTO IT, NO ONE WOULD HAVE FOUND ME – EVER.

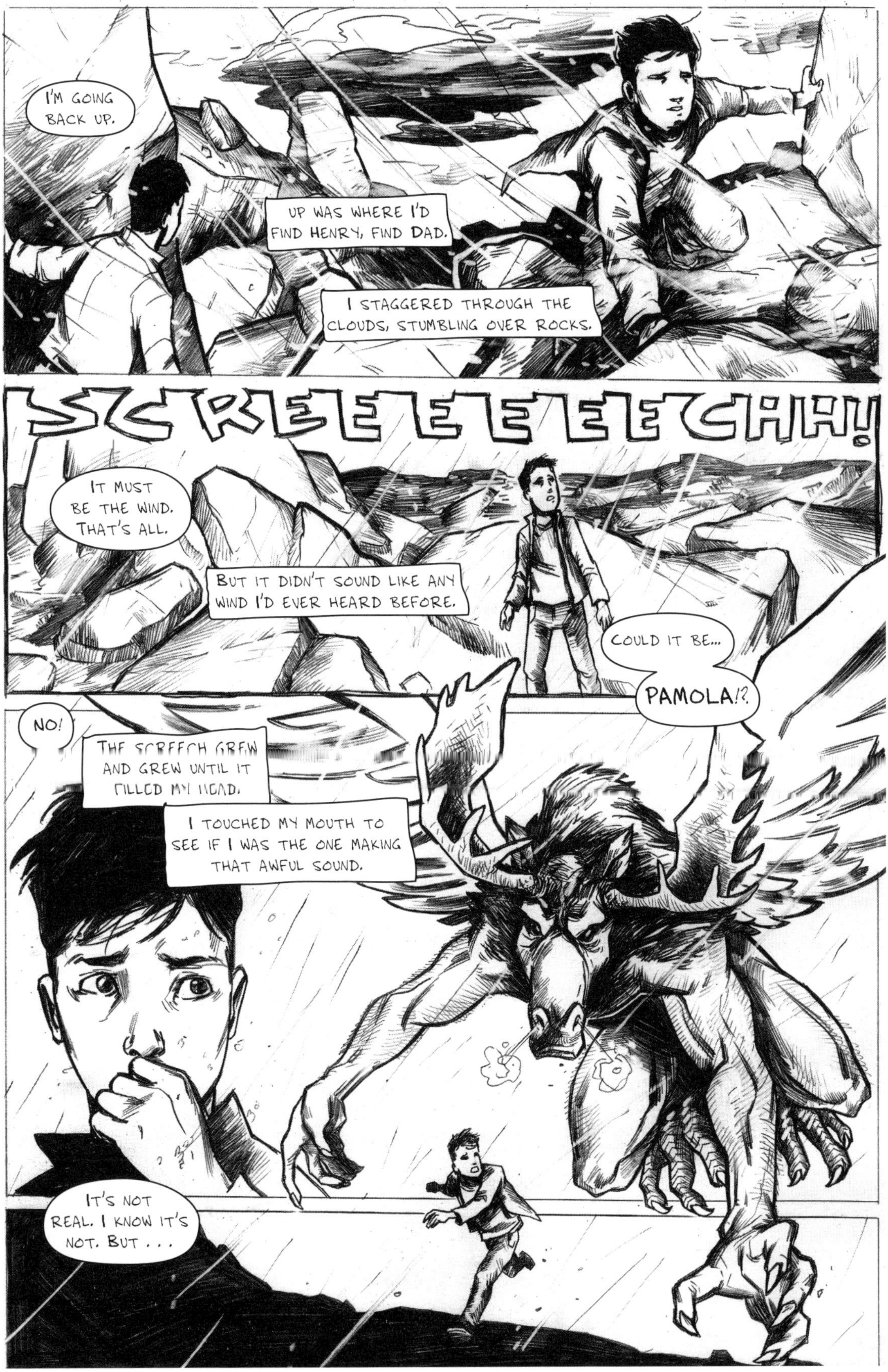
I'M GOING BACK UP.
UP WAS WHERE I'D FIND HENRY, FIND DAD.
I STAGGERED THROUGH THE CLOUDS, STUMBLING OVER ROCKS.
SCREEEEEECHH!
IT MUST BE THE WIND. THAT'S ALL.
BUT IT DIDN'T SOUND LIKE ANY WIND I'D EVER HEARD BEFORE.
COULD IT BE...
PAMOLA!?
NO!
THE SCREECH GREW AND GREW UNTIL IT FILLED MY HEAD.
I TOUCHED MY MOUTH TO SEE IF I WAS THE ONE MAKING THAT AWFUL SOUND.
IT'S NOT REAL. I KNOW IT'S NOT. BUT . . .

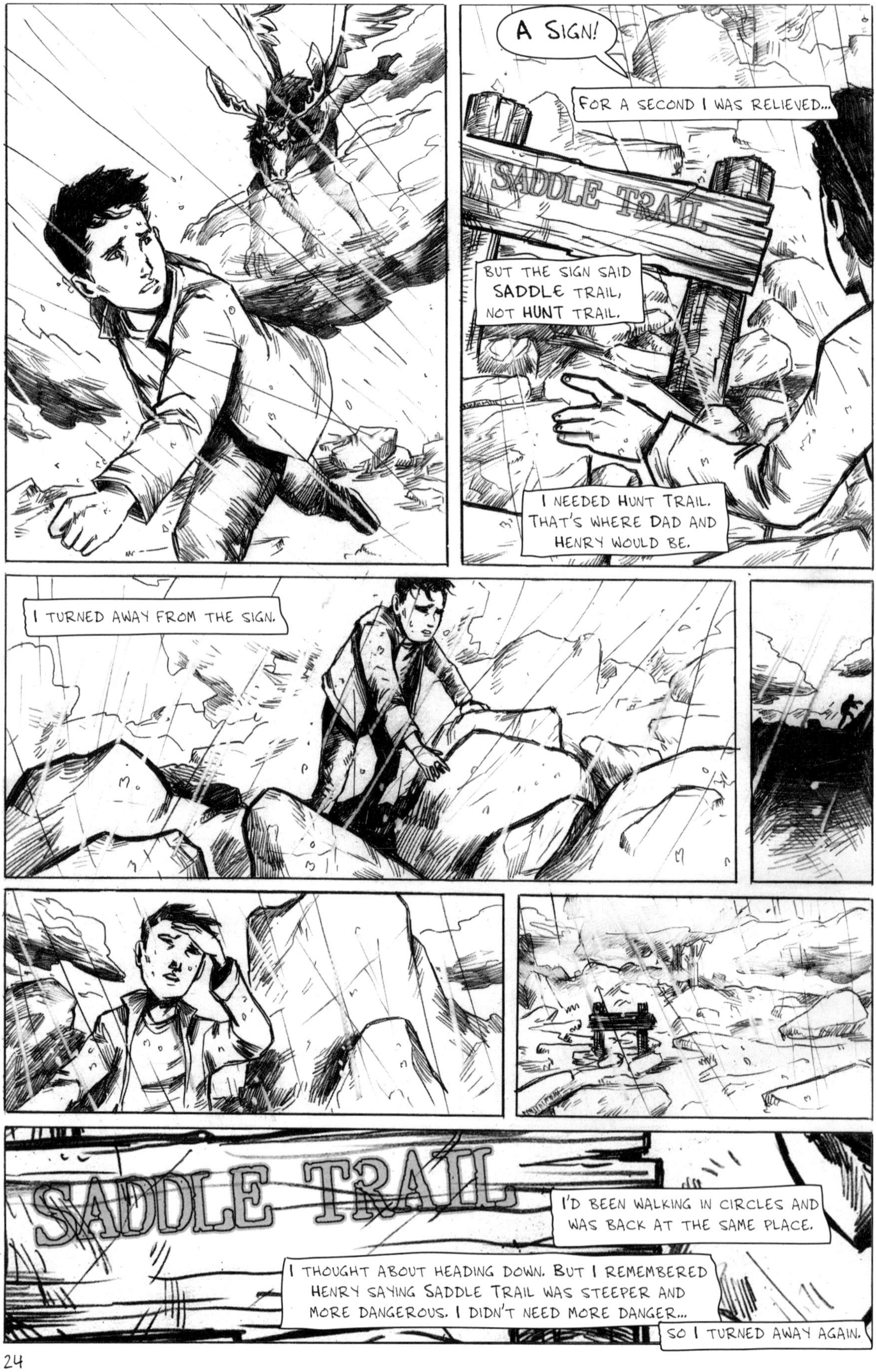
A SIGN!
FOR A SECOND I WAS RELIEVED...
SADDLE TRAIL
BUT THE SIGN SAID SADDLE TRAIL, NOT HUNT TRAIL.
I NEEDED HUNT TRAIL. THAT'S WHERE DAD AND HENRY WOULD BE.
I TURNED AWAY FROM THE SIGN.
SADDLE TRAIL
I'D BEEN WALKING IN CIRCLES AND WAS BACK AT THE SAME PLACE.
I THOUGHT ABOUT HEADING DOWN. BUT I REMEMBERED HENRY SAYING SADDLE TRAIL WAS STEEPER AND MORE DANGEROUS. I DIDN'T NEED MORE DANGER...
SO I TURNED AWAY AGAIN.

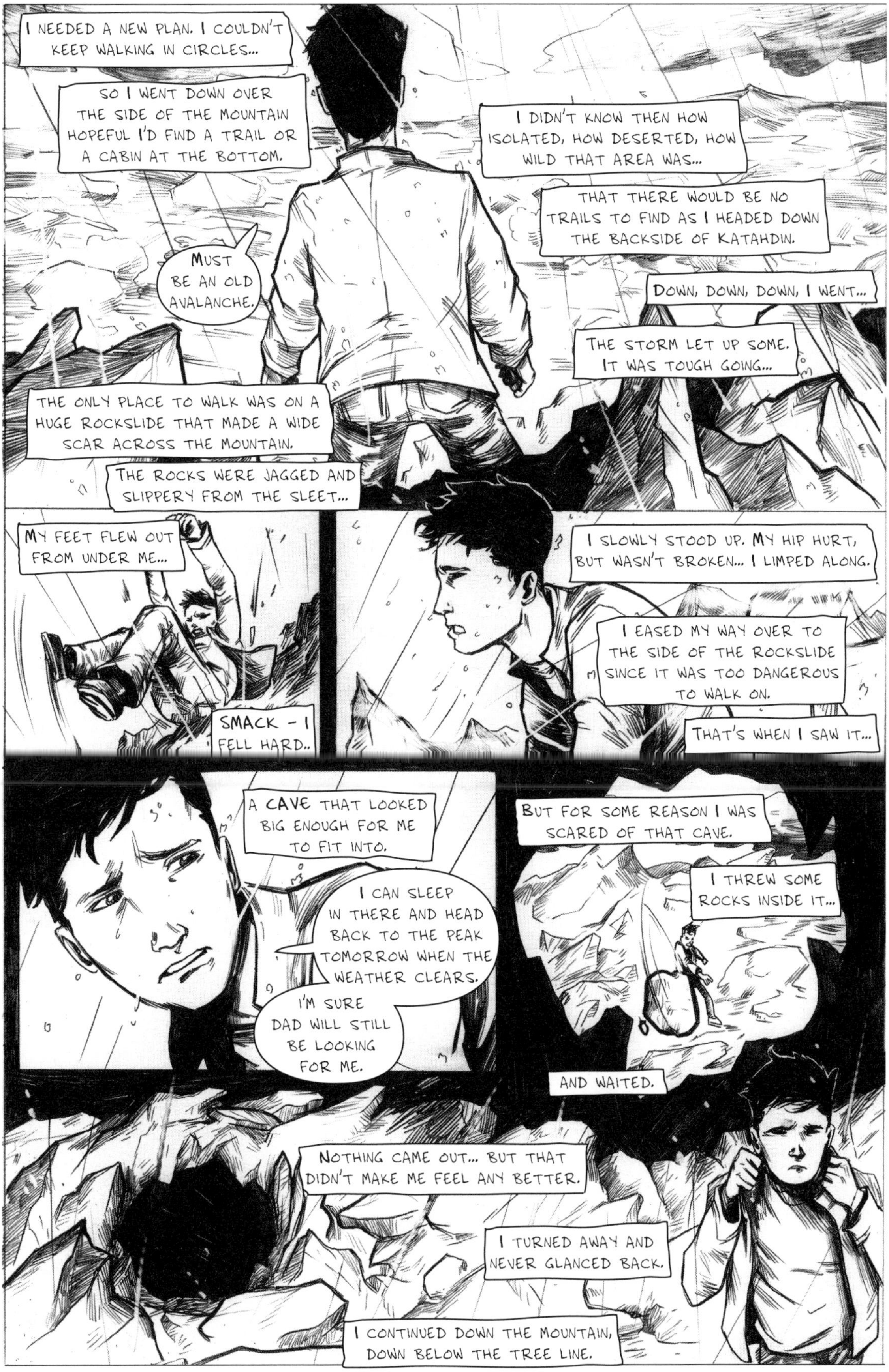
I NEEDED A NEW PLAN. I COULDN'T KEEP WALKING IN CIRCLES...
SO I WENT DOWN OVER THE SIDE OF THE MOUNTAIN HOPEFUL I'D FIND A TRAIL OR A CABIN AT THE BOTTOM.
I DIDN'T KNOW THEN HOW ISOLATED, HOW DESERTED, HOW WILD THAT AREA WAS...
THAT THERE WOULD BE NO TRAILS TO FIND AS I HEADED DOWN THE BACKSIDE OF KATAHDIN.
MUST BE AN OLD AVALANCHE.
DOWN, DOWN, DOWN, I WENT...
THE STORM LET UP SOME. IT WAS TOUGH GOING...
THE ONLY PLACE TO WALK WAS ON A HUGE ROCKSLIDE THAT MADE A WIDE SCAR ACROSS THE MOUNTAIN.
THE ROCKS WERE JAGGED AND SLIPPERY FROM THE SLEET...
MY FEET FLEW OUT FROM UNDER ME...
SMACK - I FELL HARD..
I SLOWLY STOOD UP. MY HIP HURT, BUT WASN'T BROKEN... I LIMPED ALONG.
I EASED MY WAY OVER TO THE SIDE OF THE ROCKSLIDE SINCE IT WAS TOO DANGEROUS TO WALK ON.
THAT'S WHEN I SAW IT...
A CAVE THAT LOOKED BIG ENOUGH FOR ME TO FIT INTO.
I CAN SLEEP IN THERE AND HEAD BACK TO THE PEAK TOMORROW WHEN THE WEATHER CLEARS.
I'M SURE DAD WILL STILL BE LOOKING FOR ME.
BUT FOR SOME REASON I WAS SCARED OF THAT CAVE.
I THREW SOME ROCKS INSIDE IT...
AND WAITED.
NOTHING CAME OUT... BUT THAT DIDN'T MAKE ME FEEL ANY BETTER.
I TURNED AWAY AND NEVER GLANCED BACK.
I CONTINUED DOWN THE MOUNTAIN, DOWN BELOW THE TREE LINE.

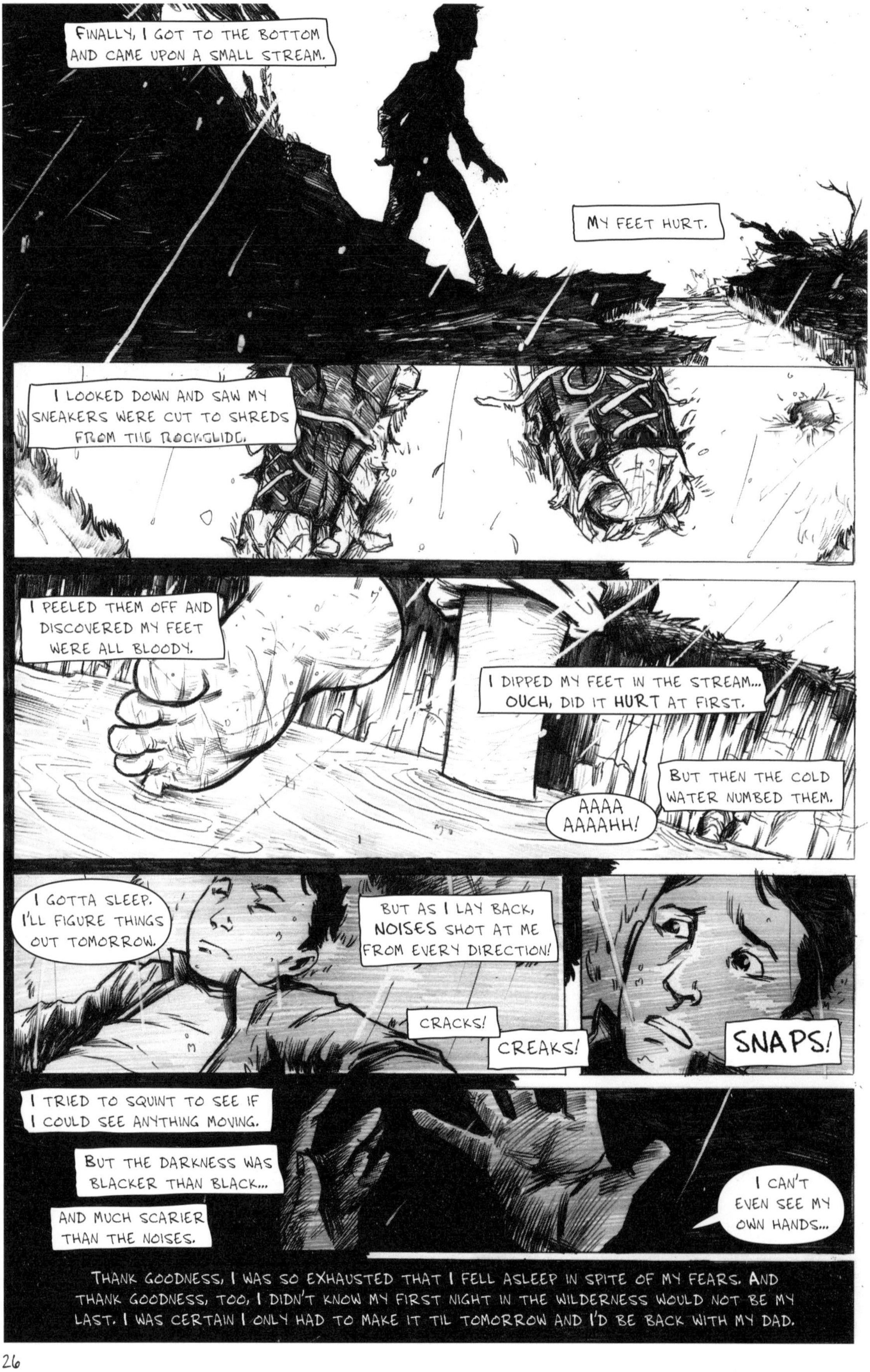
FINALLY, I GOT TO THE BOTTOM AND CAME UPON A SMALL STREAM.
MY FEET HURT.
I LOOKED DOWN AND SAW MY SNEAKERS WERE CUT TO SHREDS FROM THE ROCKSLIDE.
I PEELED THEM OFF AND DISCOVERED MY FEET WERE ALL BLOODY.
I DIPPED MY FEET IN THE STREAM... OUCH, DID IT HURT AT FIRST.
BUT THEN THE COLD WATER NUMBED THEM.
AAAA AAAAHH!
I GOTTA SLEEP. I'LL FIGURE THINGS OUT TOMORROW.
BUT AS I LAY BACK, NOISES SHOT AT ME FROM EVERY DIRECTION!
CRACKS!
CREAKS!
SNAPS!
I TRIED TO SQUINT TO SEE IF I COULD SEE ANYTHING MOVING.
BUT THE DARKNESS WAS BLACKER THAN BLACK...
AND MUCH SCARIER THAN THE NOISES.
I CAN'T EVEN SEE MY OWN HANDS...
THANK GOODNESS, I WAS SO EXHAUSTED THAT I FELL ASLEEP IN SPITE OF MY FEARS. AND THANK GOODNESS, TOO, I DIDN'T KNOW MY FIRST NIGHT IN THE WILDERNESS WOULD NOT BE MY LAST. I WAS CERTAIN I ONLY HAD TO MAKE IT TIL TOMORROW AND I'D BE BACK WITH MY DAD.

The Bangor Daily N[ews]

Tuesday, July 18, 1939

MISSING PERSON REPORTED ON MOUNT KATAHDIN

Millinocket (AP) - A late night report on Monday from the Piscataquis County Sheriff's Department told of a missing person on mile-high Mount Katahdin.

Rangers based at Baxter State Park were to start an overnight search with an expanded search to begin at daylight Tuesday if needed. Officials described stormy conditions with strong winds and frigid temperatures.

The identity of the missing person was unknown at press time. A sheriff's department spokesman said, "More details will be available on Tuesday, including, hopefully, word of a speedy and safe rescue. That mountain at night, and especially during a storm, is not fit for man or beast."

27

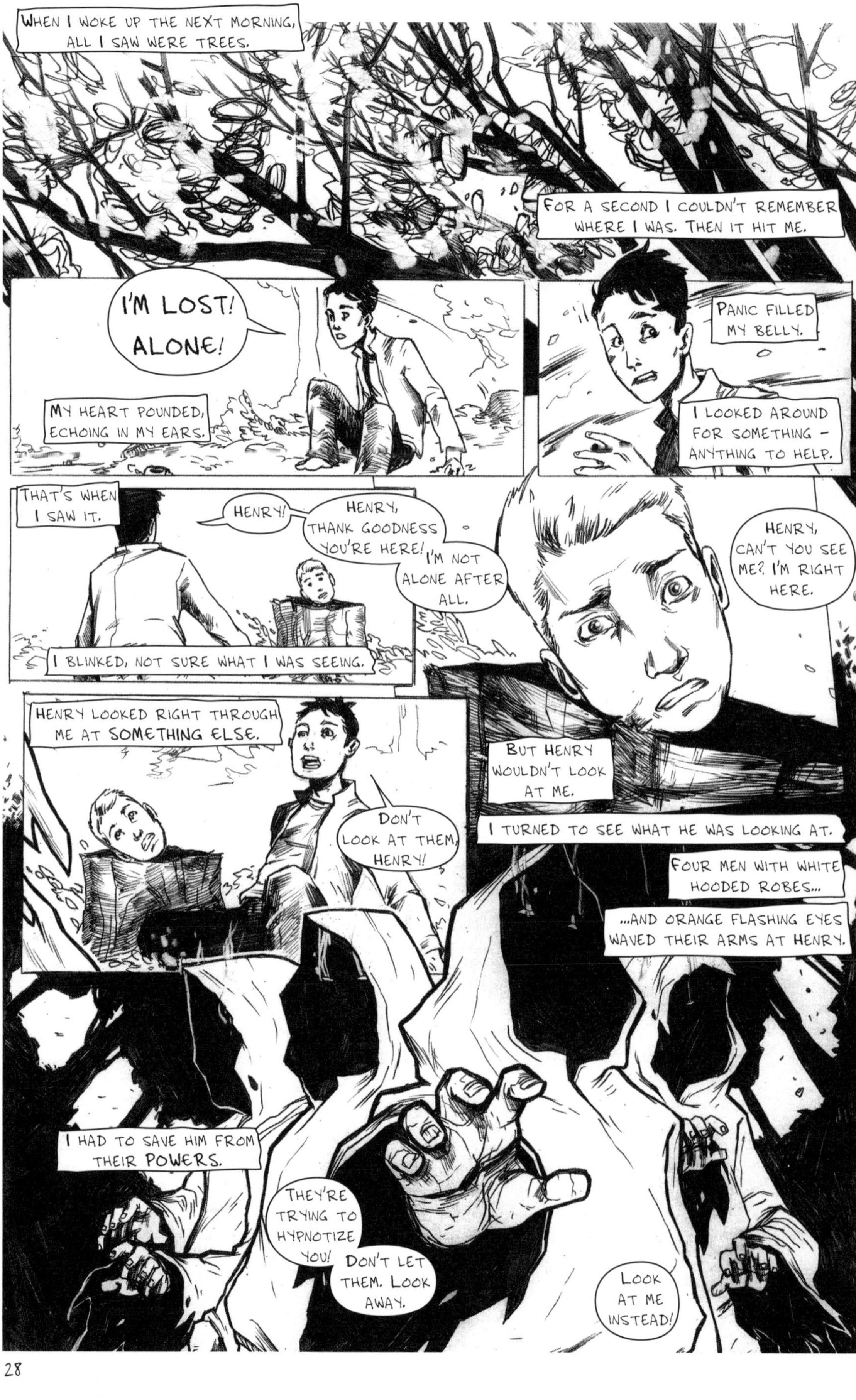
WHEN I WOKE UP THE NEXT MORNING, ALL I SAW WERE TREES.
FOR A SECOND I COULDN'T REMEMBER WHERE I WAS. THEN IT HIT ME.
I'M LOST! ALONE!
MY HEART POUNDED, ECHOING IN MY EARS.
PANIC FILLED MY BELLY.
I LOOKED AROUND FOR SOMETHING – ANYTHING TO HELP.
THAT'S WHEN I SAW IT.
HENRY!
HENRY, THANK GOODNESS YOU'RE HERE!
I'M NOT ALONE AFTER ALL.
I BLINKED, NOT SURE WHAT I WAS SEEING.
HENRY, CAN'T YOU SEE ME? I'M RIGHT HERE.
BUT HENRY WOULDN'T LOOK AT ME.
HENRY LOOKED RIGHT THROUGH ME AT SOMETHING ELSE.
DON'T LOOK AT THEM, HENRY!
I TURNED TO SEE WHAT HE WAS LOOKING AT.
FOUR MEN WITH WHITE HOODED ROBES...
...AND ORANGE FLASHING EYES WAVED THEIR ARMS AT HENRY.
I HAD TO SAVE HIM FROM THEIR POWERS.
THEY'RE TRYING TO HYPNOTIZE YOU!
DON'T LET THEM. LOOK AWAY.
LOOK AT ME INSTEAD!

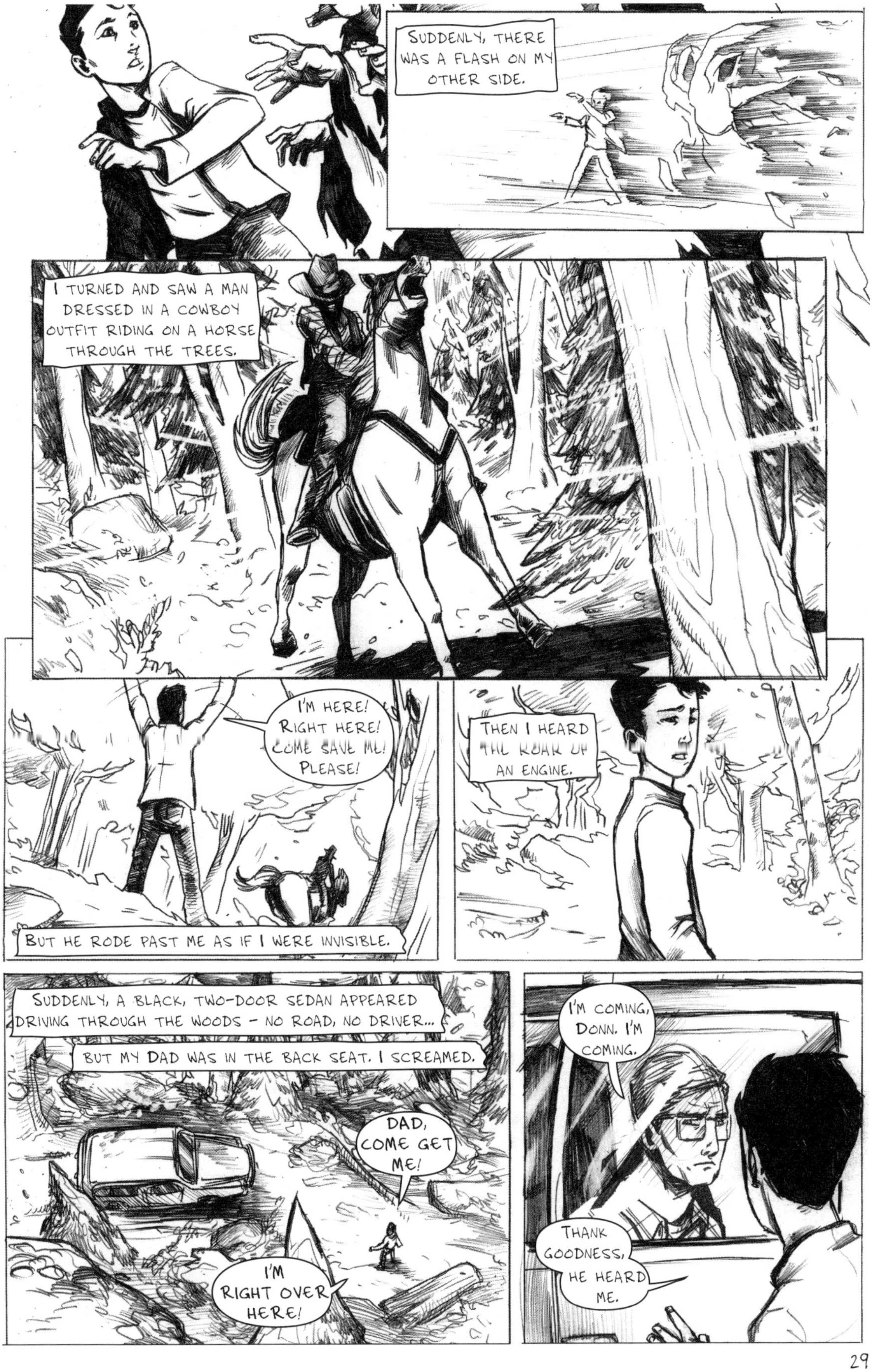

SUDDENLY, THERE WAS A FLASH ON MY OTHER SIDE.
I TURNED AND SAW A MAN DRESSED IN A COWBOY OUTFIT RIDING ON A HORSE THROUGH THE TREES.
I'M HERE! RIGHT HERE! COME SAVE ME! PLEASE!
BUT HE RODE PAST ME AS IF I WERE INVISIBLE.
THEN I HEARD THE ROAR OF AN ENGINE.
SUDDENLY, A BLACK, TWO-DOOR SEDAN APPEARED DRIVING THROUGH THE WOODS - NO ROAD, NO DRIVER...
BUT MY DAD WAS IN THE BACK SEAT. I SCREAMED.
DAD, COME GET ME!
I'M RIGHT OVER HERE!
I'M COMING, DONN. I'M COMING.
THANK GOODNESS, HE HEARD ME.

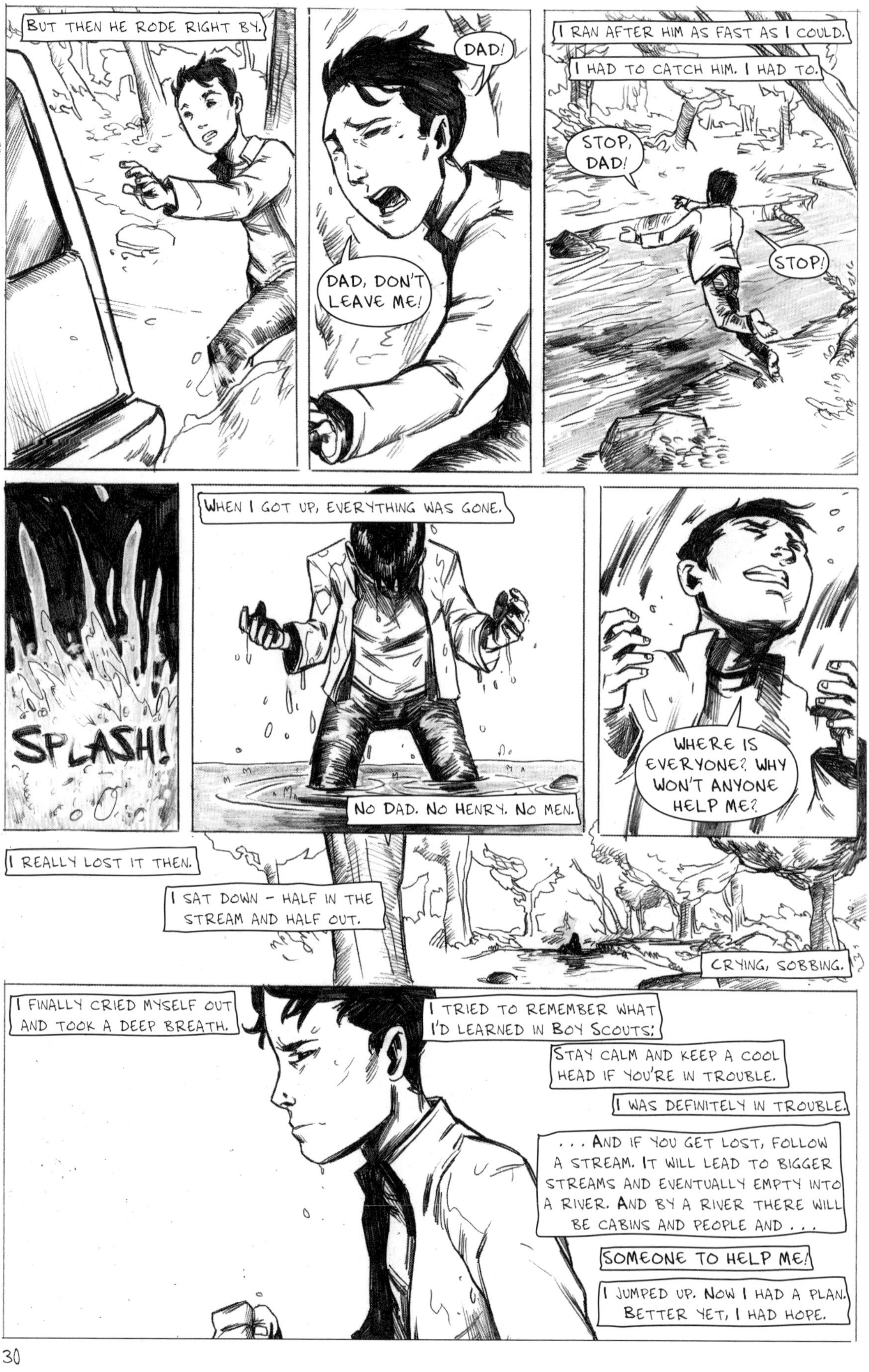

BUT THEN HE RODE RIGHT BY.
DAD!
DAD, DON'T LEAVE ME!
I RAN AFTER HIM AS FAST AS I COULD.
I HAD TO CATCH HIM. I HAD TO.
STOP, DAD!
STOP!
SPLASH!
WHEN I GOT UP, EVERYTHING WAS GONE.
NO DAD. NO HENRY. NO MEN.
WHERE IS EVERYONE? WHY WON'T ANYONE HELP ME?
I REALLY LOST IT THEN.
I SAT DOWN - HALF IN THE STREAM AND HALF OUT.
CRYING, SOBBING.
I FINALLY CRIED MYSELF OUT AND TOOK A DEEP BREATH.
I TRIED TO REMEMBER WHAT I'D LEARNED IN BOY SCOUTS:
STAY CALM AND KEEP A COOL HEAD IF YOU'RE IN TROUBLE.
I WAS DEFINITELY IN TROUBLE.
. . . AND IF YOU GET LOST, FOLLOW A STREAM. IT WILL LEAD TO BIGGER STREAMS AND EVENTUALLY EMPTY INTO A RIVER. AND BY A RIVER THERE WILL BE CABINS AND PEOPLE AND . . .
SOMEONE TO HELP ME!
I JUMPED UP. NOW I HAD A PLAN. BETTER YET, I HAD HOPE.

I GRABBED MY SNEAKERS AND STARTED TO PUT THEM ON.

OW!

MY FEET WERE SO SWOLLEN — THEY DIDN'T FIT.

THEY WERE TOO SHREDDED TO WEAR ANYWAY, SO I TIED THEM TOGETHER, SLUNG THEM OVER MY SHOULDER...

AND STARTED FOLLOWING THE STREAM.

FOLLOWING IT AROUND EVERY TWIST AND TURN...

EVERY BEND AND CROOK.

OVER BIG ROCKS AND BLOW DOWNS.

THROUGH THICK BRUSH.

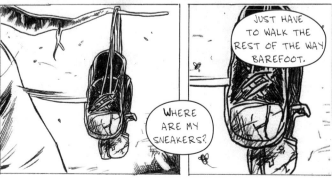
WHERE ARE MY SNEAKERS?

JUST HAVE TO WALK THE REST OF THE WAY BAREFOOT.

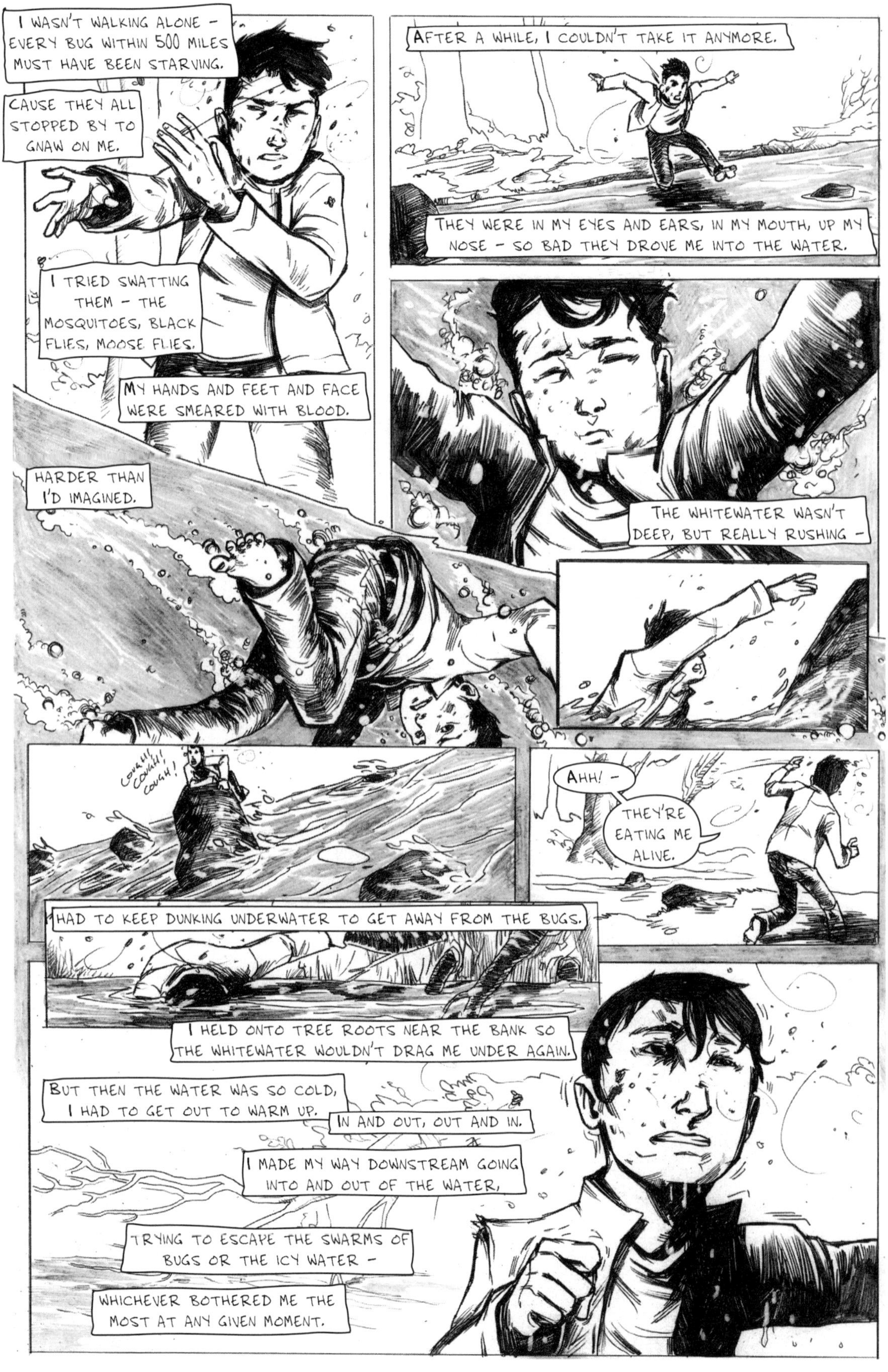
I WASN'T WALKING ALONE - EVERY BUG WITHIN 500 MILES MUST HAVE BEEN STARVING.
CAUSE THEY ALL STOPPED BY TO GNAW ON ME.
I TRIED SWATTING THEM - THE MOSQUITOES, BLACK FLIES, MOOSE FLIES.
MY HANDS AND FEET AND FACE WERE SMEARED WITH BLOOD.
AFTER A WHILE, I COULDN'T TAKE IT ANYMORE.
THEY WERE IN MY EYES AND EARS, IN MY MOUTH, UP MY NOSE - SO BAD THEY DROVE ME INTO THE WATER.
THE WHITEWATER WASN'T DEEP, BUT REALLY RUSHING -
HARDER THAN I'D IMAGINED.
COUGH! COUGH! COUGH!
AHH! -
THEY'RE EATING ME ALIVE.
HAD TO KEEP DUNKING UNDERWATER TO GET AWAY FROM THE BUGS.
I HELD ONTO TREE ROOTS NEAR THE BANK SO THE WHITEWATER WOULDN'T DRAG ME UNDER AGAIN.
BUT THEN THE WATER WAS SO COLD, I HAD TO GET OUT TO WARM UP.
IN AND OUT, OUT AND IN.
I MADE MY WAY DOWNSTREAM GOING INTO AND OUT OF THE WATER,
TRYING TO ESCAPE THE SWARMS OF BUGS OR THE ICY WATER -
WHICHEVER BOTHERED ME THE MOST AT ANY GIVEN MOMENT.

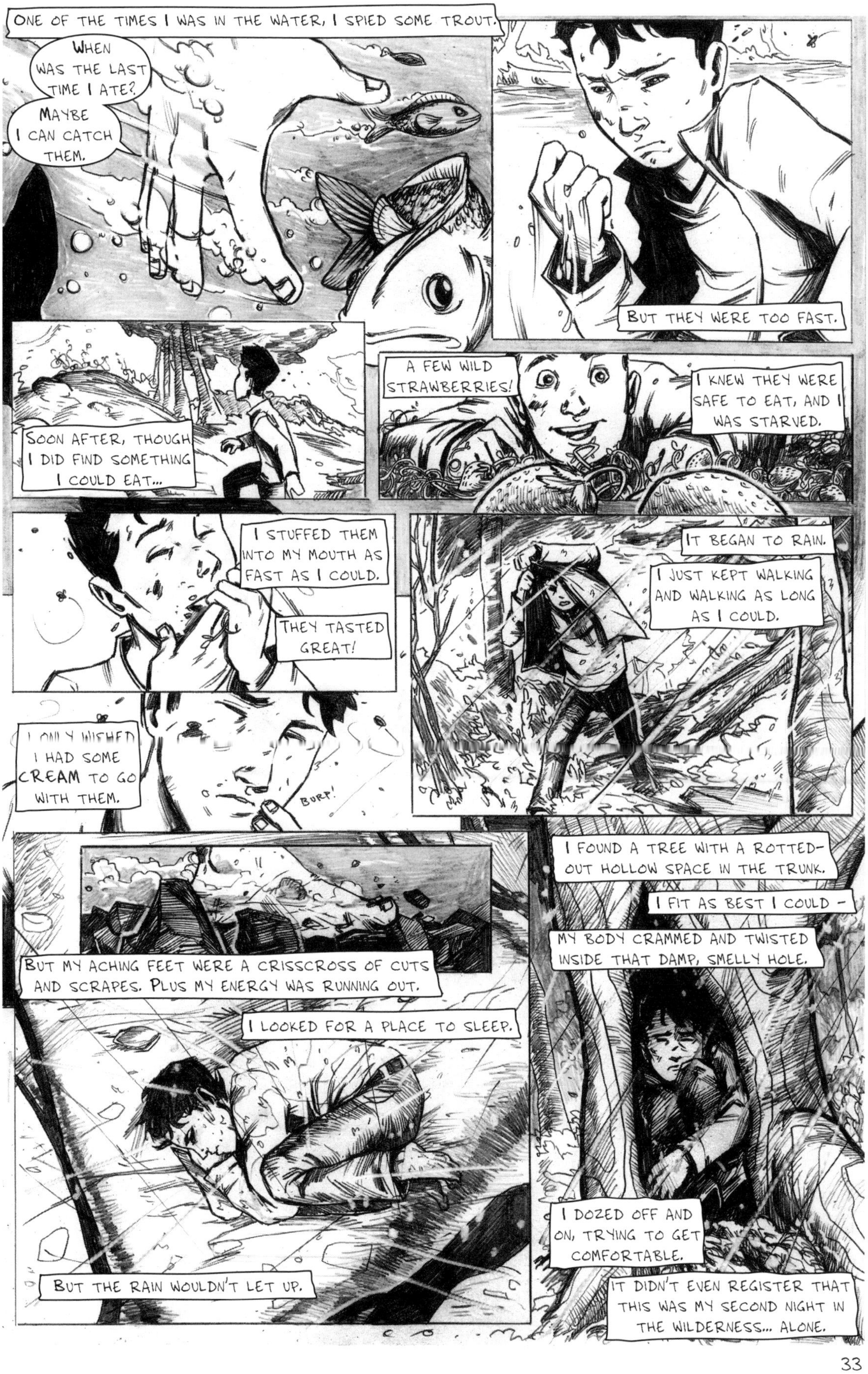
ONE OF THE TIMES I WAS IN THE WATER, I SPIED SOME TROUT.
WHEN WAS THE LAST TIME I ATE?
MAYBE I CAN CATCH THEM.
BUT THEY WERE TOO FAST.
SOON AFTER, THOUGH I DID FIND SOMETHING I COULD EAT...
A FEW WILD STRAWBERRIES!
I KNEW THEY WERE SAFE TO EAT, AND I WAS STARVED.
I STUFFED THEM INTO MY MOUTH AS FAST AS I COULD.
THEY TASTED GREAT!
I ONLY WISHED I HAD SOME CREAM TO GO WITH THEM.
BURP!
IT BEGAN TO RAIN.
I JUST KEPT WALKING AND WALKING AS LONG AS I COULD.
BUT MY ACHING FEET WERE A CRISSCROSS OF CUTS AND SCRAPES. PLUS MY ENERGY WAS RUNNING OUT.
I LOOKED FOR A PLACE TO SLEEP.
BUT THE RAIN WOULDN'T LET UP.
I FOUND A TREE WITH A ROTTED-OUT HOLLOW SPACE IN THE TRUNK.
I FIT AS BEST I COULD -
MY BODY CRAMMED AND TWISTED INSIDE THAT DAMP, SMELLY HOLE.
I DOZED OFF AND ON, TRYING TO GET COMFORTABLE.
IT DIDN'T EVEN REGISTER THAT THIS WAS MY SECOND NIGHT IN THE WILDERNESS... ALONE.

Bangor Daily News

Wednesday, July 19, 1939

12-YEAR-OLD NEW YORK BOY MISSING ON MOUNT KATAHDIN

Millinocket (AP) - Donn Fendler, a 12-year-old boy from Rye, New York, went missing on Mount Katahdin on Monday. As of late Tuesday, there was no sign of the boy.

Fifty forest rangers, sheriff deputies, and lumbermen searched throughout the day. The search was to be expanded on Wednesday into inaccessible terrain and a call went out for experienced woodsmen to join the efforts. Bloodhounds were also to be dispatched on Wednesday, hoping to find the boy's scent.

Tuesday's search was concentrated near the Hunt Trail where young Fendler was last seen hiking with family and friends Monday afternoon before getting separated from them during a sudden storm on the mountain.

The boy's father, Mr. Donald Fendler, was reported to be helping in the search after sending his other sons back to Mrs. Fendler at the family's vacation cabin in Newport.

Mr. Fendler said that his son, Donn, "has a good head on his shoulders and some Boy Scout training which should help him in the wilds." Mr. Fendler also expressed his appreciation for the searchers' efforts. "With the help of all these good folks, Donn will be back with us soon, very soon."

IN THE MORNING, WHEN I TUMBLED OUT OF THAT TREE, I WAS SO STIFF I COULD BARELY STAND.

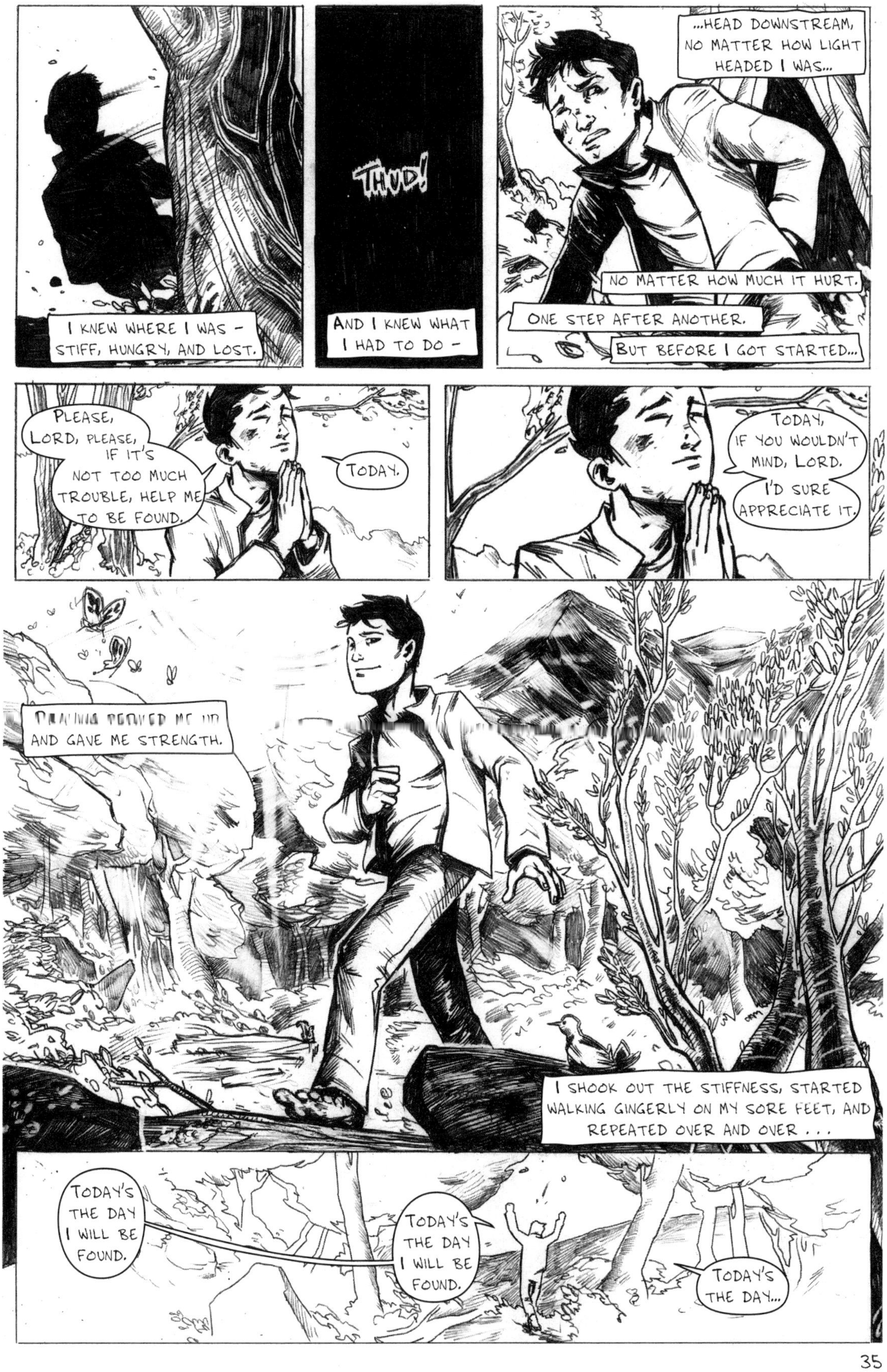
I KNEW WHERE I WAS - STIFF, HUNGRY, AND LOST.
THUD!
AND I KNEW WHAT I HAD TO DO -
...HEAD DOWNSTREAM, NO MATTER HOW LIGHT HEADED I WAS...
NO MATTER HOW MUCH IT HURT.
ONE STEP AFTER ANOTHER.
BUT BEFORE I GOT STARTED...
PLEASE, LORD, PLEASE, IF IT'S NOT TOO MUCH TROUBLE, HELP ME TO BE FOUND.
TODAY.
TODAY, IF YOU WOULDN'T MIND, LORD.
I'D SURE APPRECIATE IT.
AND GAVE ME STRENGTH.
I SHOOK OUT THE STIFFNESS, STARTED WALKING GINGERLY ON MY SORE FEET, AND REPEATED OVER AND OVER . . .
TODAY'S THE DAY I WILL BE FOUND.
TODAY'S THE DAY I WILL BE FOUND.
TODAY'S THE DAY...

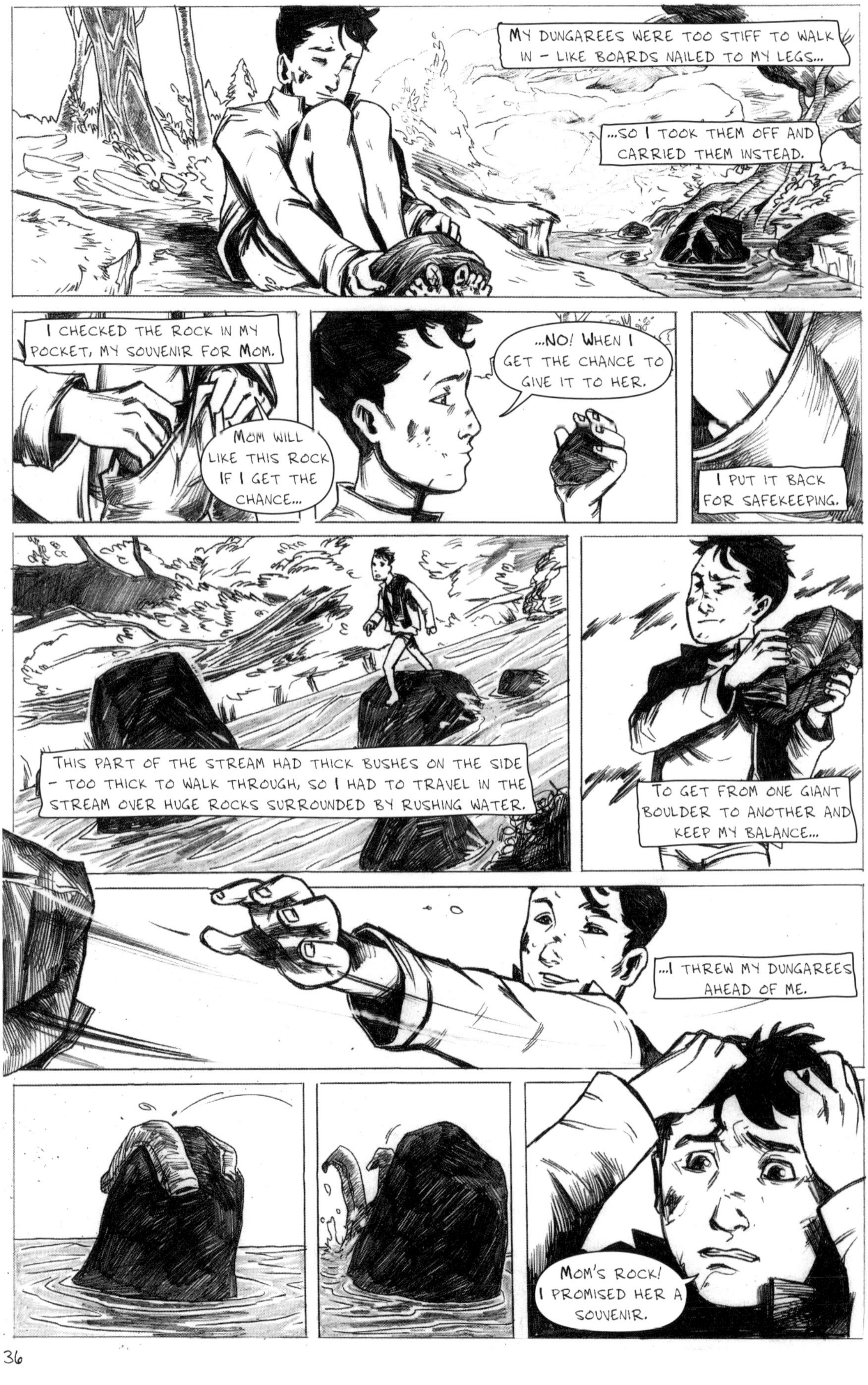
MY DUNGAREES WERE TOO STIFF TO WALK IN – LIKE BOARDS NAILED TO MY LEGS...
...SO I TOOK THEM OFF AND CARRIED THEM INSTEAD.
I CHECKED THE ROCK IN MY POCKET, MY SOUVENIR FOR MOM.
MOM WILL LIKE THIS ROCK IF I GET THE CHANCE...
...NO! WHEN I GET THE CHANCE TO GIVE IT TO HER.
I PUT IT BACK FOR SAFEKEEPING.
THIS PART OF THE STREAM HAD THICK BUSHES ON THE SIDE – TOO THICK TO WALK THROUGH, SO I HAD TO TRAVEL IN THE STREAM OVER HUGE ROCKS SURROUNDED BY RUSHING WATER.
TO GET FROM ONE GIANT BOULDER TO ANOTHER AND KEEP MY BALANCE...
...I THREW MY DUNGAREES AHEAD OF ME.
MOM'S ROCK! I PROMISED HER A SOUVENIR.

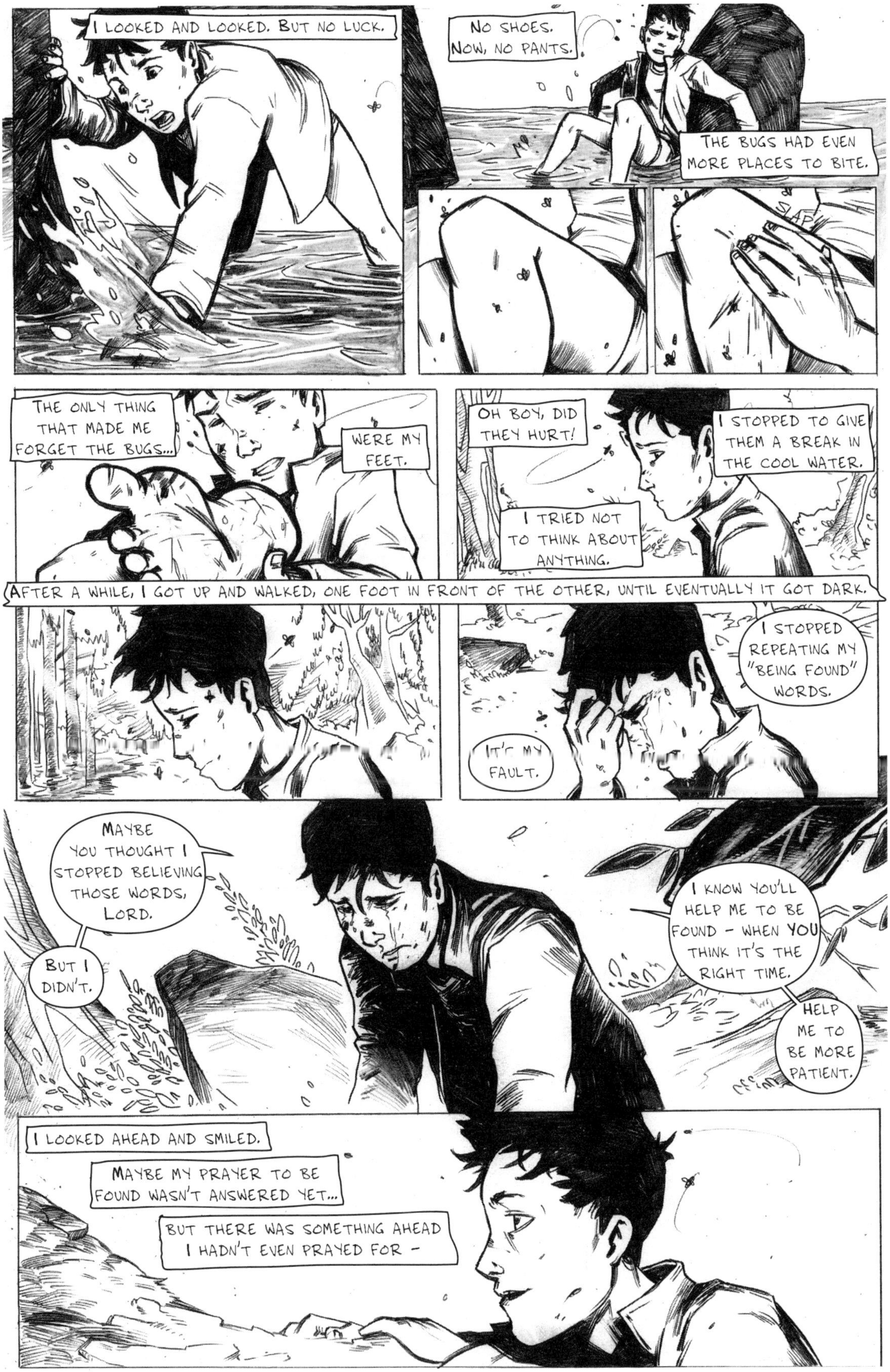
I LOOKED AND LOOKED. BUT NO LUCK.
NO SHOES. NOW, NO PANTS.
THE BUGS HAD EVEN MORE PLACES TO BITE.
SLAP!
THE ONLY THING THAT MADE ME FORGET THE BUGS...
WERE MY FEET.
OH BOY, DID THEY HURT!
I STOPPED TO GIVE THEM A BREAK IN THE COOL WATER.
I TRIED NOT TO THINK ABOUT ANYTHING.
AFTER A WHILE, I GOT UP AND WALKED, ONE FOOT IN FRONT OF THE OTHER, UNTIL EVENTUALLY IT GOT DARK.
I STOPPED REPEATING MY "BEING FOUND" WORDS.
IT'S MY FAULT.
MAYBE YOU THOUGHT I STOPPED BELIEVING THOSE WORDS, LORD.
BUT I DIDN'T.
I KNOW YOU'LL HELP ME TO BE FOUND - WHEN YOU THINK IT'S THE RIGHT TIME.
HELP ME TO BE MORE PATIENT.
I LOOKED AHEAD AND SMILED.
MAYBE MY PRAYER TO BE FOUND WASN'T ANSWERED YET...
BUT THERE WAS SOMETHING AHEAD I HADN'T EVEN PRAYED FOR -

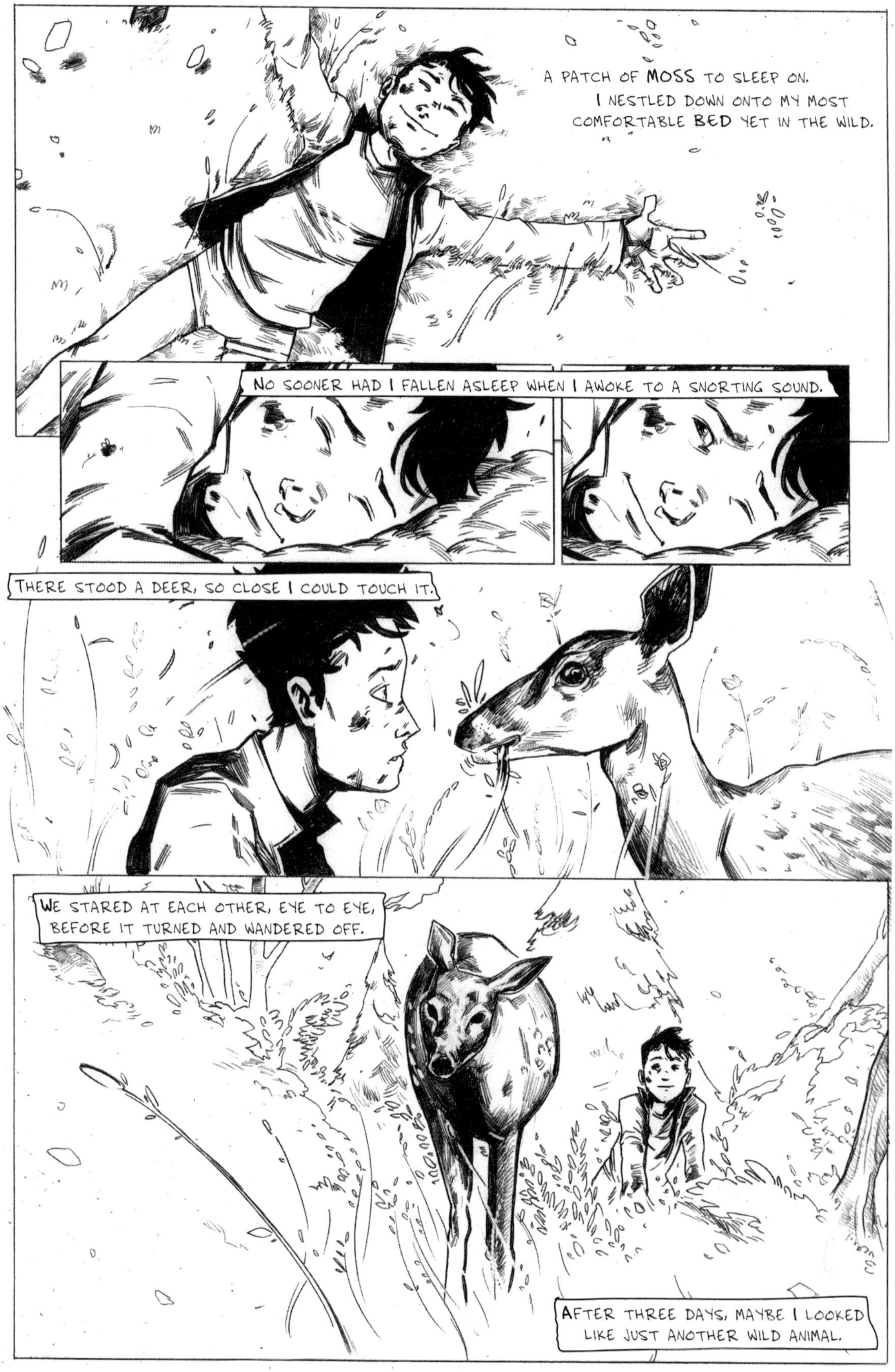
A PATCH OF MOSS TO SLEEP ON.
I NESTLED DOWN ONTO MY MOST COMFORTABLE BED YET IN THE WILD.
NO SOONER HAD I FALLEN ASLEEP WHEN I AWOKE TO A SNORTING SOUND.
THERE STOOD A DEER, SO CLOSE I COULD TOUCH IT.
WE STARED AT EACH OTHER, EYE TO EYE, BEFORE IT TURNED AND WANDERED OFF.
AFTER THREE DAYS, MAYBE I LOOKED LIKE JUST ANOTHER WILD ANIMAL.

The Bangor Daily N[

Thursday, July 20, 1939

LOST BOY'S TRACKS FOUND NEAR PRECIPITOUS DROP

Millinocket (AP) - The first sign of missing 12-year-old Donn Fendler came during Wednesday's expanded search on Mount Katahdin. The boy's shoeprints were found at the edge of Saddle Slide, a 400-foot drop above a rocky ravine.

Bloodhounds tracked the boy's scent to the edge of the precipitous drop, but were not able to track farther. Sharp rocks cut the dogs' paws so severely that it was believed one of the dogs would have to have a leg amputated. Two new bloodhounds from New York, Fendler's home state, were scheduled to arrive late Wednesday by monoplane to replace the Maine search dogs. The new dogs would continue the search on Thursday at Saddle Slide while wearing specially made leather shoes to protect their paws.

More than 100 searchers combed the mountain on Wednesday. Additional volunteers were expected to join the effort on Thursday, including some with ropes who could be lowered down the rocky slide.

When asked about the boy's chances of surviving a fall down Saddle Slide, veteran Maine Guide Roy Dudley answered that it was "faintly possible." After being told of the location of the boy's tracks, Mr. Donald Fendler, the boy's father, said, "I'm trying to make myself believe there's still a thread of hope."

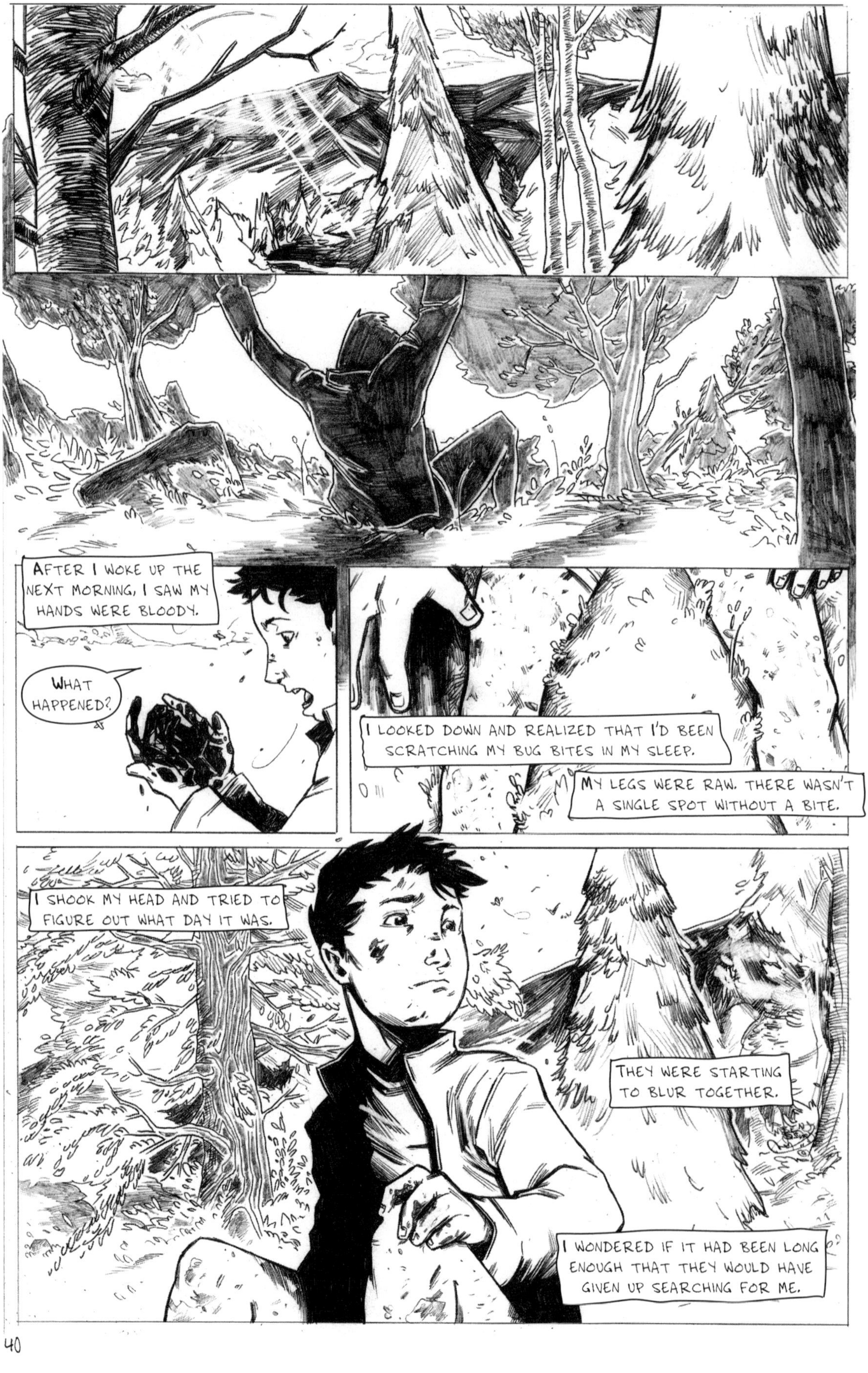

After I woke up the next morning, I saw my hands were bloody.
What happened?
I looked down and realized that I'd been scratching my bug bites in my sleep.
My legs were raw. There wasn't a single spot without a bite.
I shook my head and tried to figure out what day it was.
They were starting to blur together.
I wondered if it had been long enough that they would have given up searching for me.

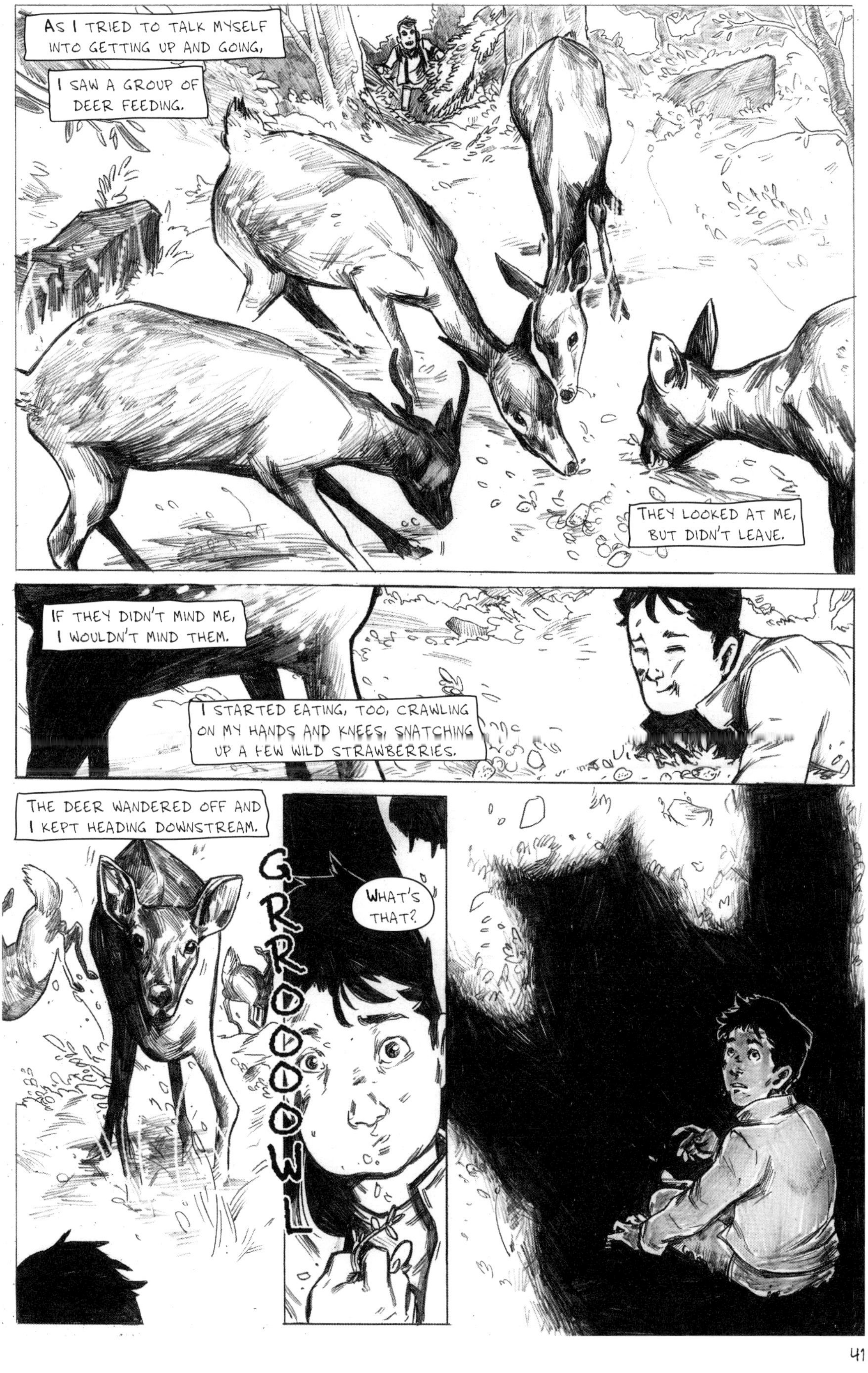

AS I TRIED TO TALK MYSELF INTO GETTING UP AND GOING,
I SAW A GROUP OF DEER FEEDING.
THEY LOOKED AT ME, BUT DIDN'T LEAVE.
IF THEY DIDN'T MIND ME, I WOULDN'T MIND THEM.
I STARTED EATING, TOO, CRAWLING ON MY HANDS AND KNEES, SNATCHING UP A FEW WILD STRAWBERRIES.
THE DEER WANDERED OFF AND I KEPT HEADING DOWNSTREAM.
GRROOOOOWL
WHAT'S THAT?

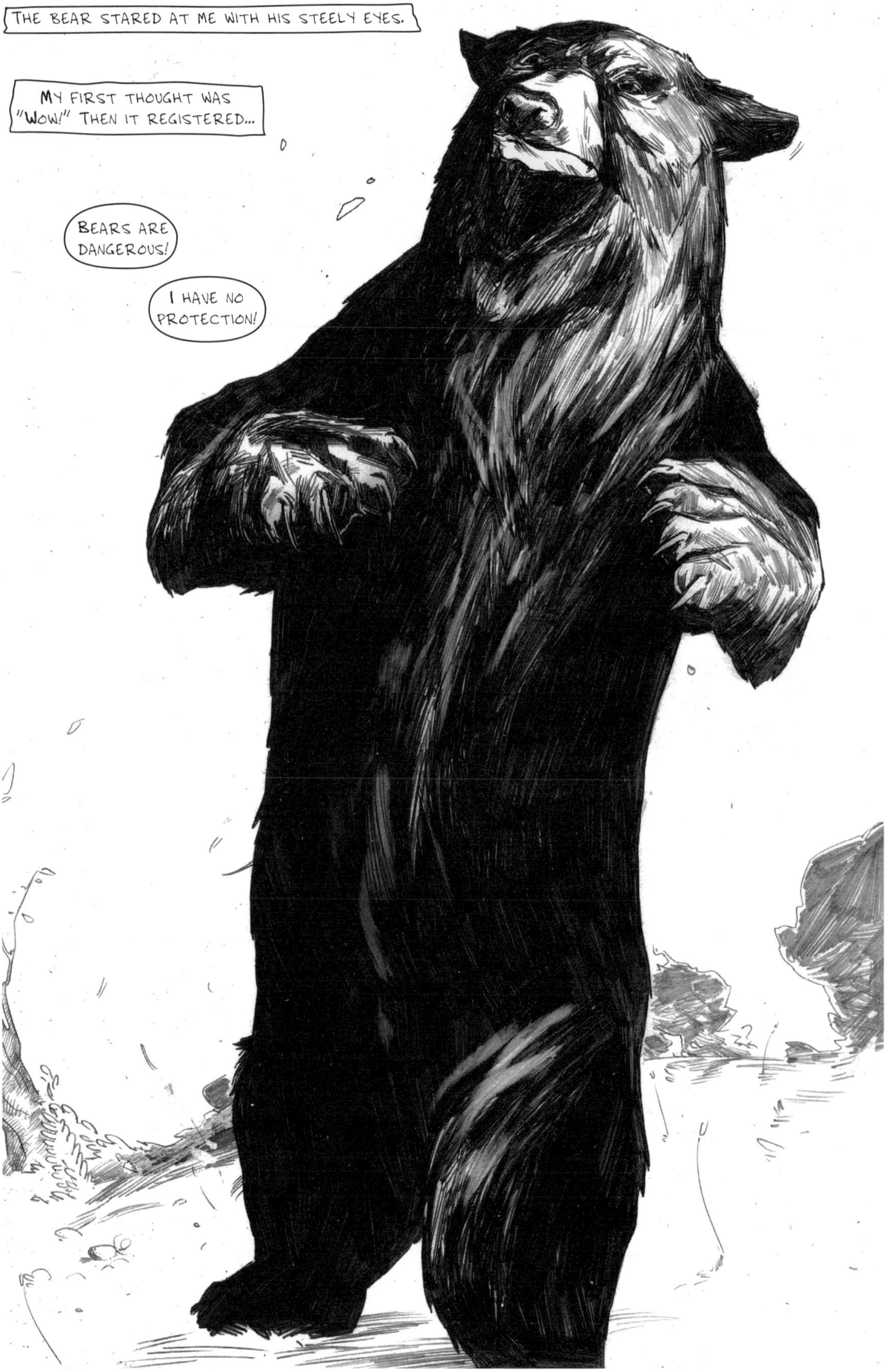
THE BEAR STARED AT ME WITH HIS STEELY EYES.
MY FIRST THOUGHT WAS "WOW!" THEN IT REGISTERED...
BEARS ARE DANGEROUS!
I HAVE NO PROTECTION!

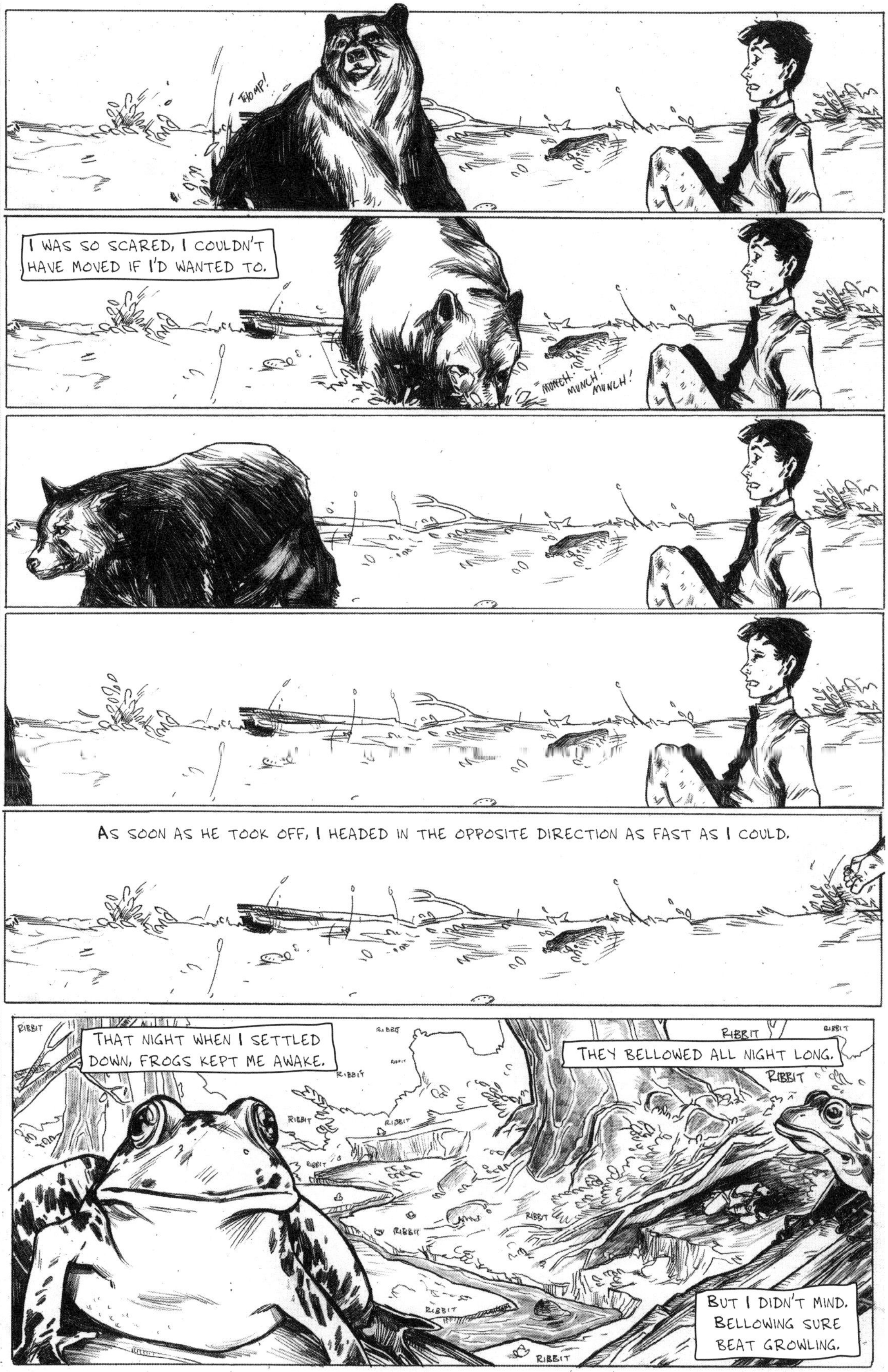
THOMP!
I WAS SO SCARED, I COULDN'T HAVE MOVED IF I'D WANTED TO.
MUNCH! MUNCH! MUNCH!
AS SOON AS HE TOOK OFF, I HEADED IN THE OPPOSITE DIRECTION AS FAST AS I COULD.
RIBBIT
THAT NIGHT WHEN I SETTLED DOWN, FROGS KEPT ME AWAKE.
RIBBIT
THEY BELLOWED ALL NIGHT LONG.
RIBBIT
RIBBIT
RIBBIT
BUT I DIDN'T MIND. BELLOWING SURE BEAT GROWLING.
RIBBIT

angor Daily

Friday, July 21, 1939

SEARCH EXPANDS FOR LOST BOY, NEW TRACKS FOUND

Millinocket (AP) - More than 200 searchers have joined the efforts on Mount Katahdin to find missing Donn Fendler, a seventh grader from Resurrection School in Rye, New York. Governor Lewis O. Barrows ordered National Guardsmen to join rangers, lumberers, volunteers, and Great Northern Paper Company workers.

Bloodhounds discovered a new set of tracks for the boy on Thursday. The tracks were found at the bottom of an avalanche path near Abol Stream.

A state forestry plane also joined the search on Thursday without success. The plane was called back after weather conditions deteriorated and the mountain clouded in. The forestry service hoped to try the plane once again when the weather improved.

More efforts were made Thursday to support exhausted searchers. A field kitchen and tents were set up in the middle of the mountain to offer searchers food and a place to rest.

Attempts to contact the boy's father, Donald Fendler, were unsuccessful. He, along with an uncle of young Fendler, was reportedly searching deep in the wilderness alongside other searchers.

EACH DAY IT WAS GETTING HARDER AND HARDER TO GET UP AND GET MOVING. I DREADED DAYBREAK – IT ONLY MEANT MORE PAIN, MORE HUNGER, AND THE FEAR THAT I WAS WALKING IN THE WRONG DIRECTION – AWAY FROM CIVILIZATION.

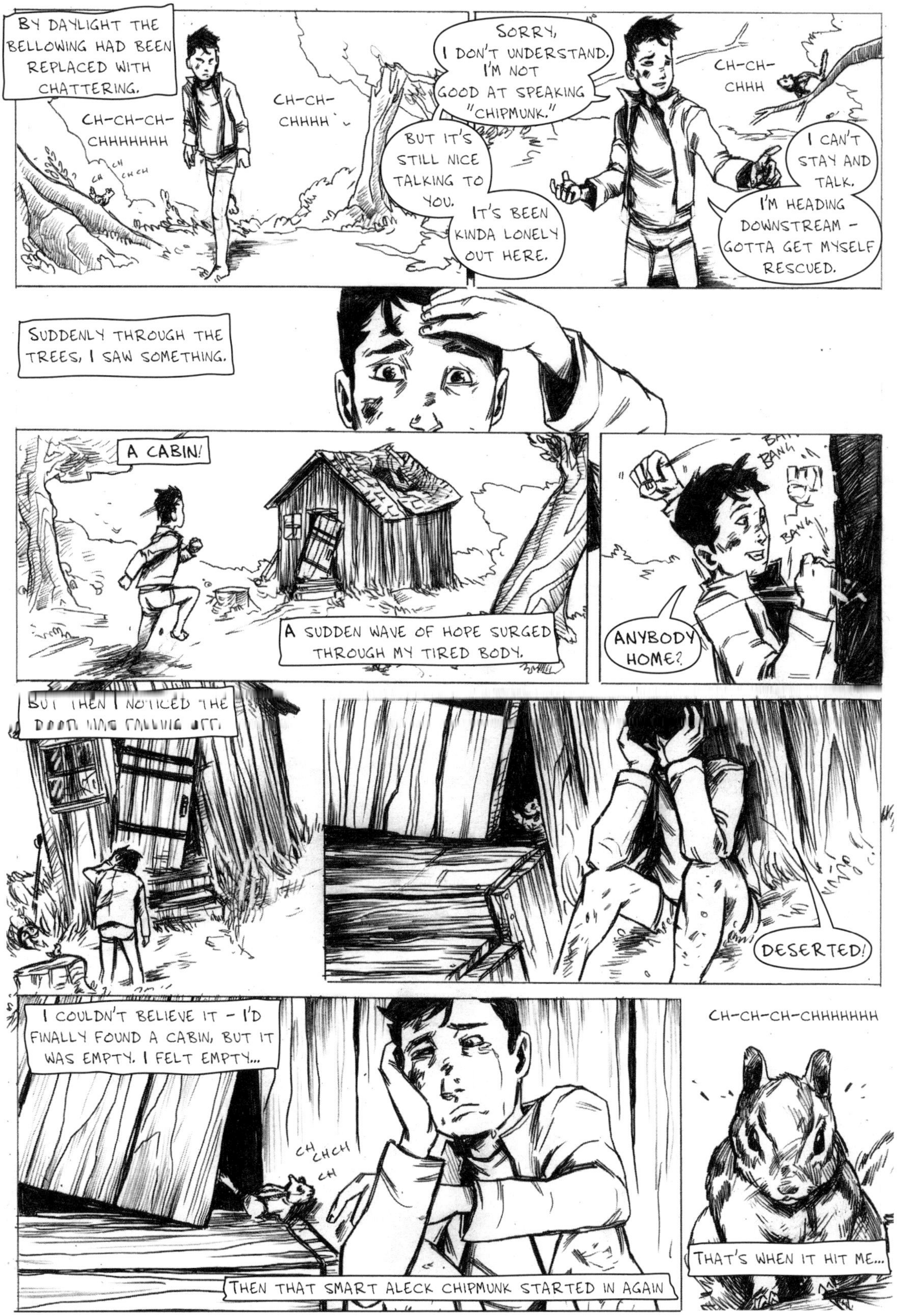

BY DAYLIGHT THE BELLOWING HAD BEEN REPLACED WITH CHATTERING.
CH-CH-CH-CHHHHHHH
CH-CH-CHHHH
SORRY, I DON'T UNDERSTAND. I'M NOT GOOD AT SPEAKING "CHIPMUNK."
BUT IT'S STILL NICE TALKING TO YOU.
IT'S BEEN KINDA LONELY OUT HERE.
CH-CH-CHHH
I CAN'T STAY AND TALK.
I'M HEADING DOWNSTREAM – GOTTA GET MYSELF RESCUED.
SUDDENLY THROUGH THE TREES, I SAW SOMETHING.
A CABIN!
A SUDDEN WAVE OF HOPE SURGED THROUGH MY TIRED BODY.
BANG
BANG
ANYBODY HOME?
BUT THEN I NOTICED THE DOOR WAS FALLING OFF.
DESERTED!
I COULDN'T BELIEVE IT – I'D FINALLY FOUND A CABIN, BUT IT WAS EMPTY. I FELT EMPTY...
CH CHCH CH
THEN THAT SMART ALECK CHIPMUNK STARTED IN AGAIN
CH-CH-CH-CHHHHHHH
THAT'S WHEN IT HIT ME...

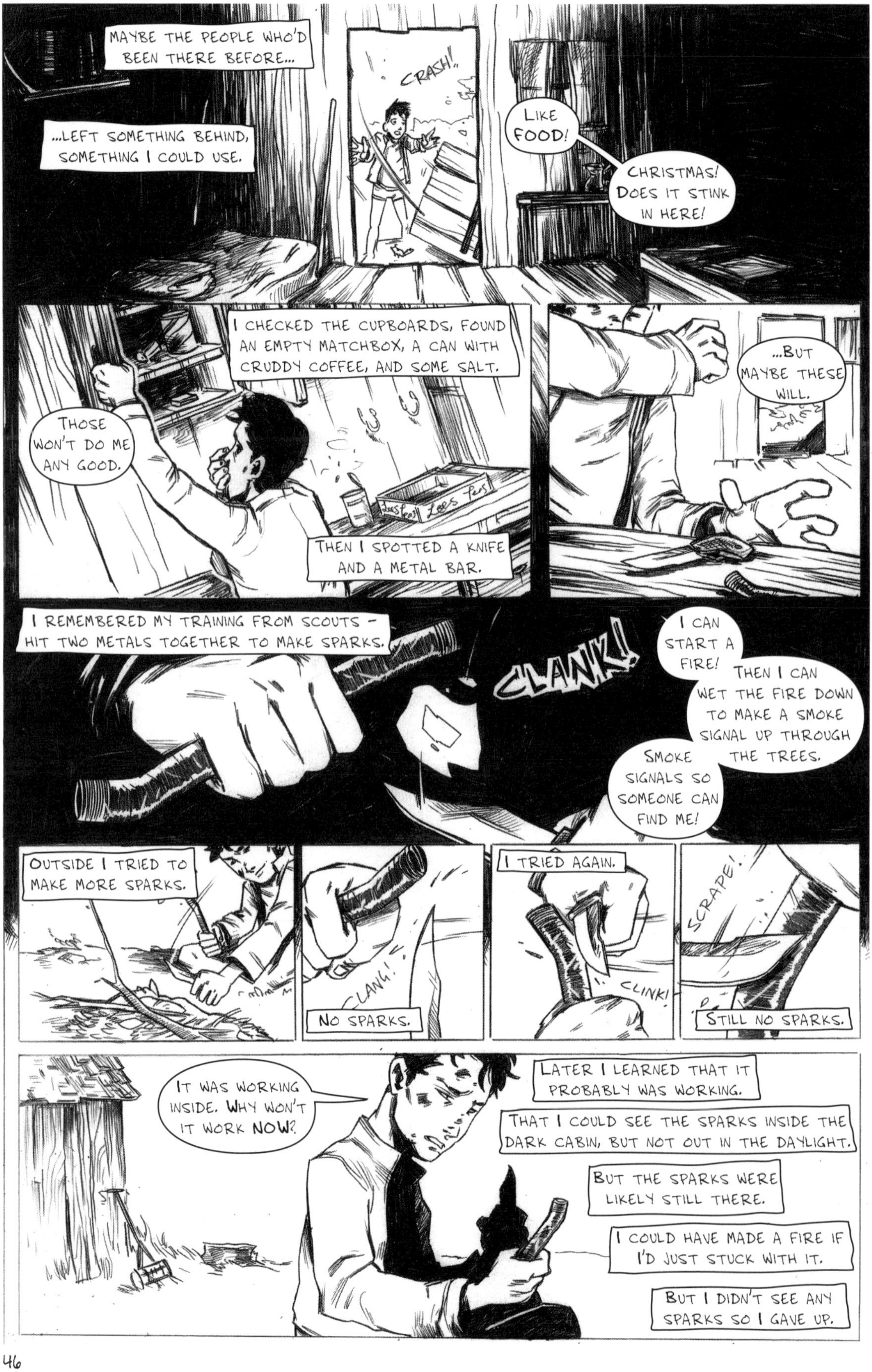
MAYBE THE PEOPLE WHO'D BEEN THERE BEFORE...
...LEFT SOMETHING BEHIND, SOMETHING I COULD USE.
CRASH!
LIKE FOOD!
CHRISTMAS! DOES IT STINK IN HERE!
I CHECKED THE CUPBOARDS, FOUND AN EMPTY MATCHBOX, A CAN WITH CRUDDY COFFEE, AND SOME SALT.
THOSE WON'T DO ME ANY GOOD.
THEN I SPOTTED A KNIFE AND A METAL BAR.
...BUT MAYBE THESE WILL.
I REMEMBERED MY TRAINING FROM SCOUTS - HIT TWO METALS TOGETHER TO MAKE SPARKS.
CLANK!
I CAN START A FIRE!
THEN I CAN WET THE FIRE DOWN TO MAKE A SMOKE SIGNAL UP THROUGH THE TREES.
SMOKE SIGNALS SO SOMEONE CAN FIND ME!
OUTSIDE I TRIED TO MAKE MORE SPARKS.
CLANK!
NO SPARKS.
I TRIED AGAIN.
CLINK!
SCRAPE!
STILL NO SPARKS.
IT WAS WORKING INSIDE. WHY WON'T IT WORK NOW?
LATER I LEARNED THAT IT PROBABLY WAS WORKING.
THAT I COULD SEE THE SPARKS INSIDE THE DARK CABIN, BUT NOT OUT IN THE DAYLIGHT.
BUT THE SPARKS WERE LIKELY STILL THERE.
I COULD HAVE MADE A FIRE IF I'D JUST STUCK WITH IT.
BUT I DIDN'T SEE ANY SPARKS SO I GAVE UP.

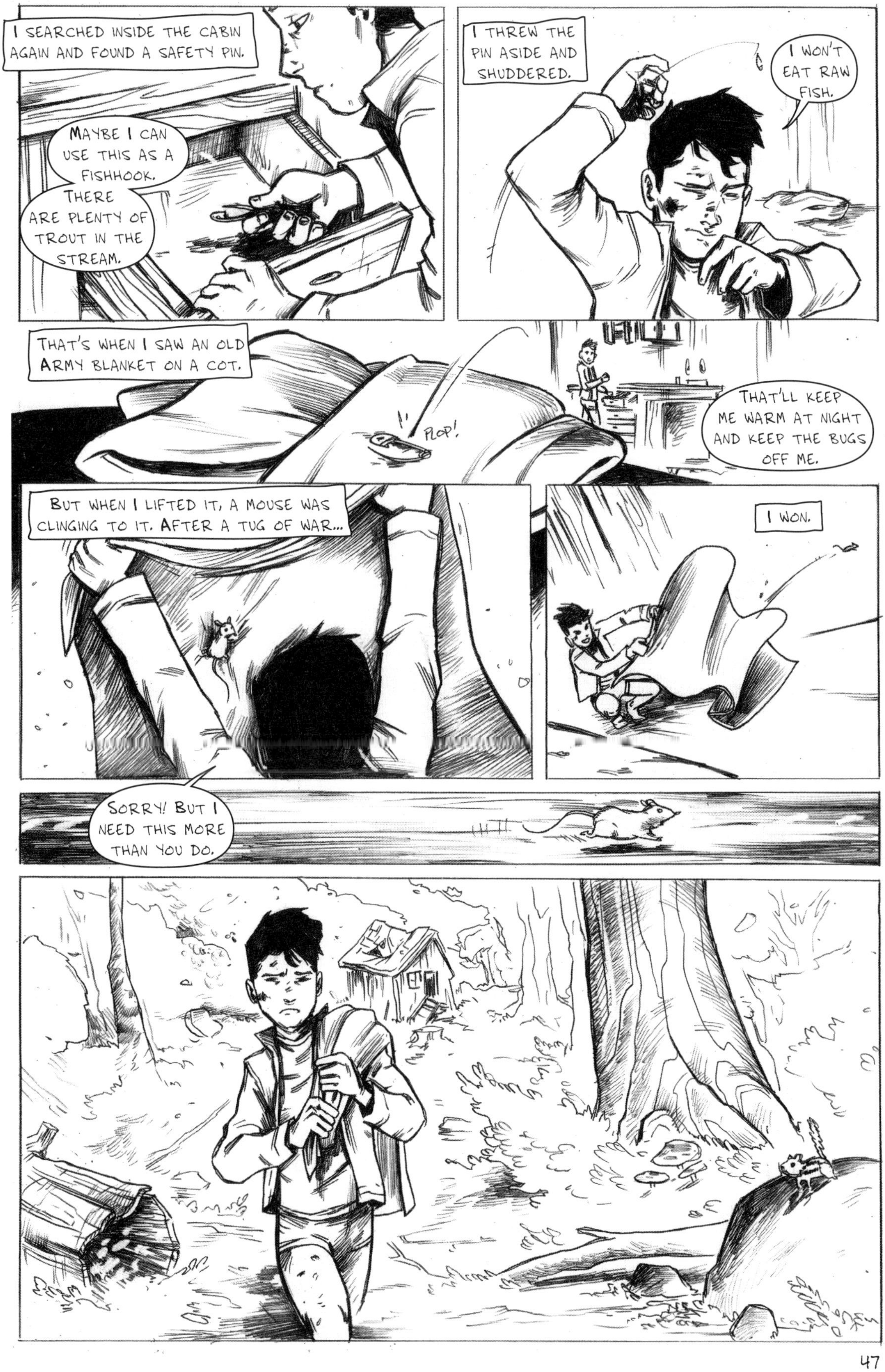
I SEARCHED INSIDE THE CABIN AGAIN AND FOUND A SAFETY PIN.
MAYBE I CAN USE THIS AS A FISHHOOK.
THERE ARE PLENTY OF TROUT IN THE STREAM.
I THREW THE PIN ASIDE AND SHUDDERED.
I WON'T EAT RAW FISH.
THAT'S WHEN I SAW AN OLD ARMY BLANKET ON A COT.
PLOP!
THAT'LL KEEP ME WARM AT NIGHT AND KEEP THE BUGS OFF ME.
BUT WHEN I LIFTED IT, A MOUSE WAS CLINGING TO IT. AFTER A TUG OF WAR...
I WON.
SORRY! BUT I NEED THIS MORE THAN YOU DO.

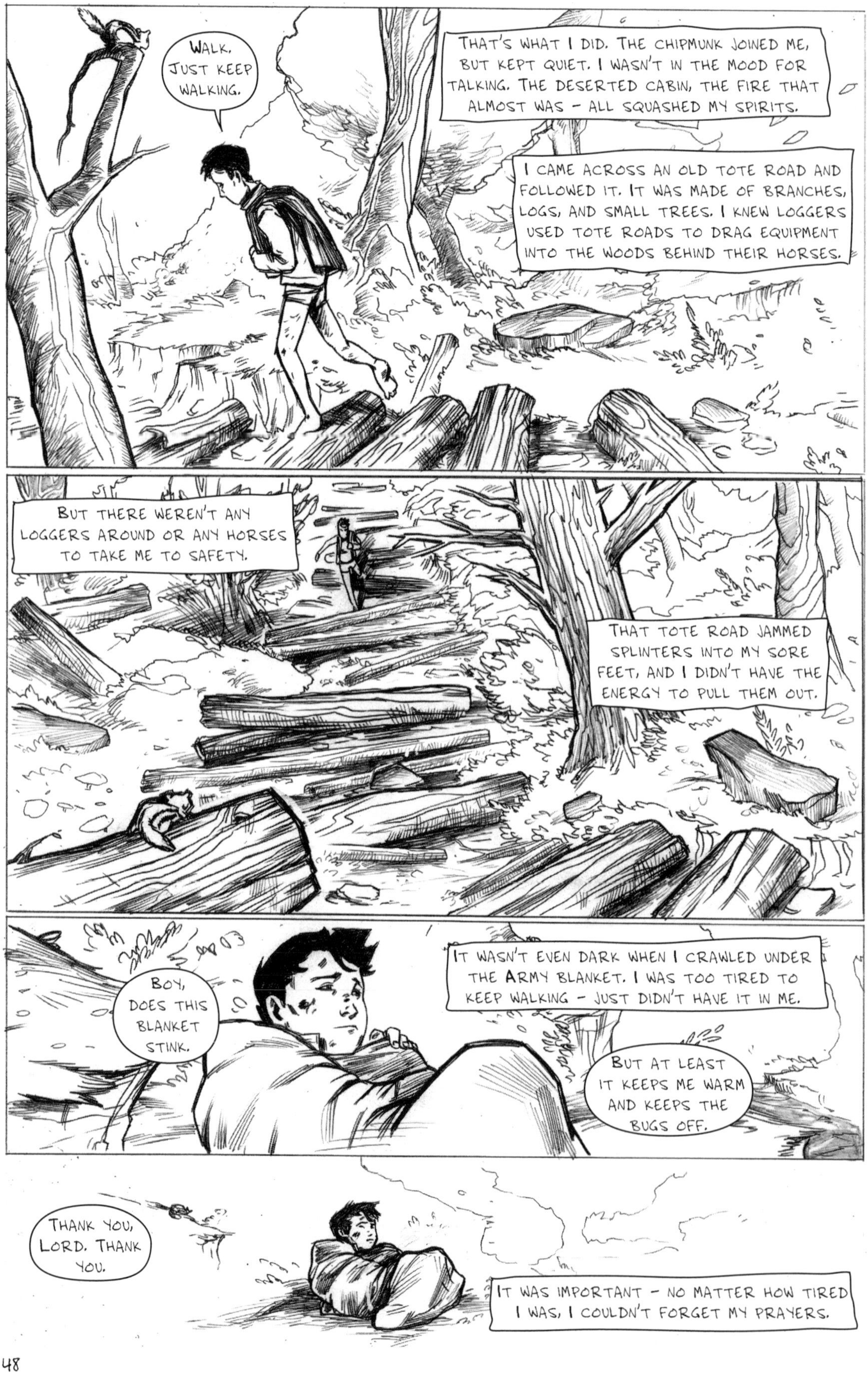
WALK. JUST KEEP WALKING.
THAT'S WHAT I DID. THE CHIPMUNK JOINED ME, BUT KEPT QUIET. I WASN'T IN THE MOOD FOR TALKING. THE DESERTED CABIN, THE FIRE THAT ALMOST WAS - ALL SQUASHED MY SPIRITS.
I CAME ACROSS AN OLD TOTE ROAD AND FOLLOWED IT. IT WAS MADE OF BRANCHES, LOGS, AND SMALL TREES. I KNEW LOGGERS USED TOTE ROADS TO DRAG EQUIPMENT INTO THE WOODS BEHIND THEIR HORSES.
BUT THERE WEREN'T ANY LOGGERS AROUND OR ANY HORSES TO TAKE ME TO SAFETY.
THAT TOTE ROAD JAMMED SPLINTERS INTO MY SORE FEET, AND I DIDN'T HAVE THE ENERGY TO PULL THEM OUT.
IT WASN'T EVEN DARK WHEN I CRAWLED UNDER THE ARMY BLANKET. I WAS TOO TIRED TO KEEP WALKING - JUST DIDN'T HAVE IT IN ME.
BOY, DOES THIS BLANKET STINK.
BUT AT LEAST IT KEEPS ME WARM AND KEEPS THE BUGS OFF.
THANK YOU, LORD. THANK YOU.
IT WAS IMPORTANT - NO MATTER HOW TIRED I WAS, I COULDN'T FORGET MY PRAYERS.

or Daily New

Saturday, July 22, 1939

HOPE FADES FOR FINDING BOY

Millinocket (AP) - The tracks belonging to 12-year-old Donn Fendler that brought searchers so much hope on Thursday faded to despair on Friday. Bloodhounds returning to the site on Friday were unable to "catch a scent" for the boy. Searchers believe the boy's scent was either too old or was lost as he moved in and out of Abol Stream.

Governor Barrows' office described the search as "likely the most exhaustive in Maine history, with 400 searchers who were determined to leave no stone unturned on that vast mountain." The governor's office has received "calls of concern from across the country as the plight of young Fendler has touched the hearts of parents from sea to shining sea."

More supplies for searchers were moved up the mountain on Friday in a most unusual fashion. Miss Anna Beaulieu, a volunteer and experienced horseman, led three horses, each packing 150 pounds of supplies, up to the makeshift camp set up mid-mountain to feed rescuers.

Mr. Donald Fendler, the boy's father, was once again unavailable for comment. Friends of Mr. Fendler did report that he was doing his best to maintain his spirits and "simply wanted the search to reveal (young) Donn's truth. Not knowing was the hard part."

BY THE TIME I WOKE UP, MORNING HAD TURNED TO AFTERNOON.

OUCH!

I SQUINTED UP AT THE SUN AND ROLLED OVER TO GET AWAY FROM IT.

I MUST HAVE KICKED THE BLANKET OFF WHEN THE DAY GREW WARM AND HAD GOTTEN A BAD SUNBURN.

DOESN'T MATTER. KEEP MOVING, DONN. JUST KEEP MOVING.

H CH CH!

THE CHIPMUNK WAS STILL THERE AND FOLLOWED ME AGAIN.

I CAN'T GO ANY FASTER.

VRRRRRRRRRRRRRR

WHAT'S THAT?

IT GREW LOUDER.

WAS I IMAGINING THINGS AGAIN? EVERYTHING SEEMED SO FUZZY.

I TRIED TO SHAKE THE COBWEBS OUT OF MY HEAD.

SOUNDS LIKE A PLANE!

IVRRRRRRRRRRRRRRRRR

IT WAS A PLANE!

I HAD TO FIND AN OPEN SPOT THROUGH THE TREES SO I COULD SEE IT. SO THE PILOT COULD SEE ME!

HERE! I'M HERE.

RIGHT HERE!

LOOK DOWN!

PLEASE! PLEEEEEEEASE!

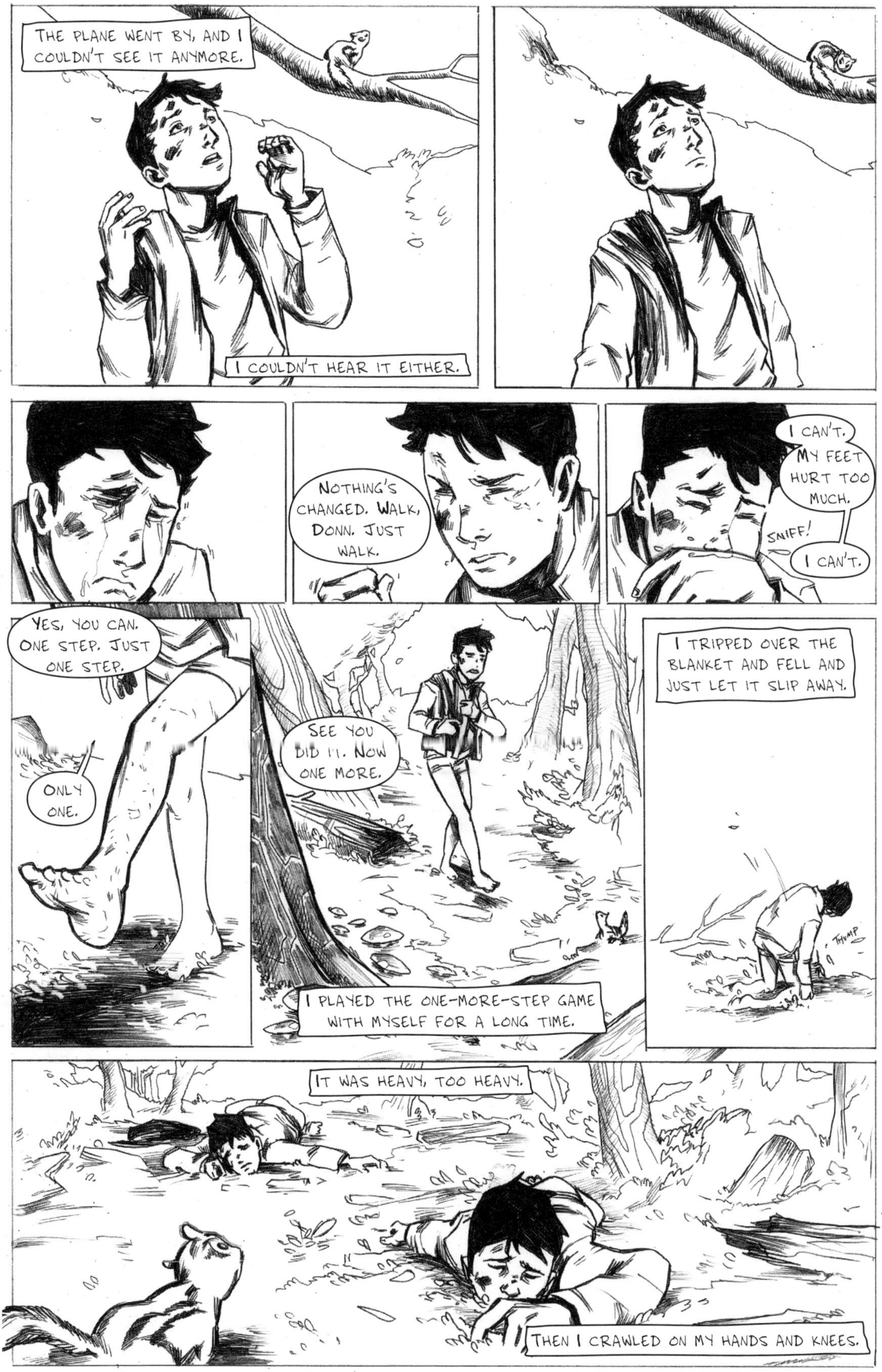

THE PLANE WENT BY, AND I COULDN'T SEE IT ANYMORE.
I COULDN'T HEAR IT EITHER.
NOTHING'S CHANGED. WALK, DONN. JUST WALK.
I CAN'T. MY FEET HURT TOO MUCH.
SNIFF!
I CAN'T.
YES, YOU CAN. ONE STEP. JUST ONE STEP.
ONLY ONE.
SEE YOU DID IT. NOW ONE MORE.
I PLAYED THE ONE-MORE-STEP GAME WITH MYSELF FOR A LONG TIME.
I TRIPPED OVER THE BLANKET AND FELL AND JUST LET IT SLIP AWAY.
THUMP
IT WAS HEAVY, TOO HEAVY.
THEN I CRAWLED ON MY HANDS AND KNEES.

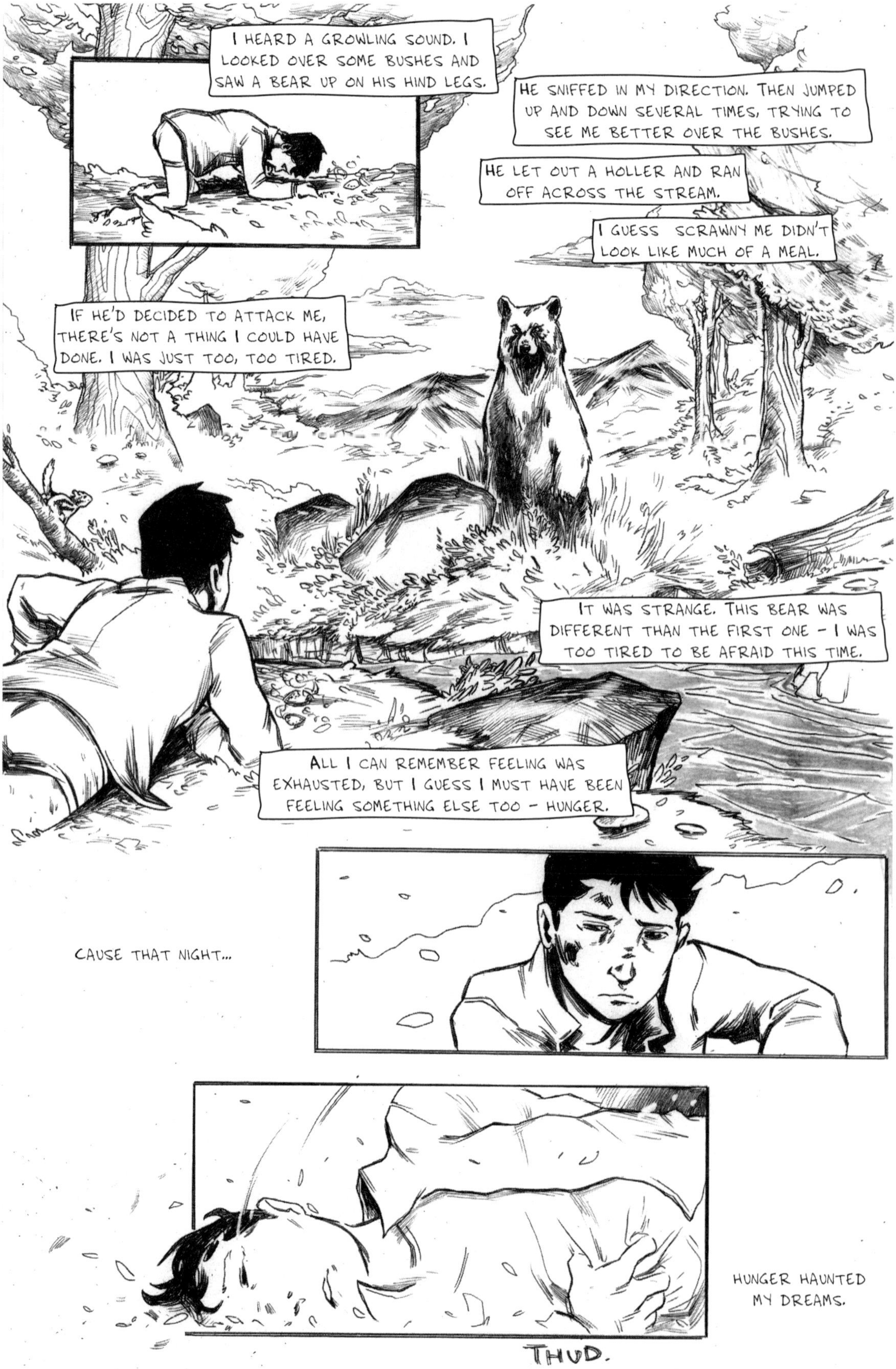
I HEARD A GROWLING SOUND. I LOOKED OVER SOME BUSHES AND SAW A BEAR UP ON HIS HIND LEGS.
HE SNIFFED IN MY DIRECTION. THEN JUMPED UP AND DOWN SEVERAL TIMES, TRYING TO SEE ME BETTER OVER THE BUSHES.
HE LET OUT A HOLLER AND RAN OFF ACROSS THE STREAM.
I GUESS SCRAWNY ME DIDN'T LOOK LIKE MUCH OF A MEAL.
IF HE'D DECIDED TO ATTACK ME, THERE'S NOT A THING I COULD HAVE DONE. I WAS JUST TOO, TOO TIRED.
IT WAS STRANGE. THIS BEAR WAS DIFFERENT THAN THE FIRST ONE - I WAS TOO TIRED TO BE AFRAID THIS TIME.
ALL I CAN REMEMBER FEELING WAS EXHAUSTED, BUT I GUESS I MUST HAVE BEEN FEELING SOMETHING ELSE TOO - HUNGER.
CAUSE THAT NIGHT...
HUNGER HAUNTED MY DREAMS.
THUD.

DAY SEVEN

SLEEP HELPED. BUT I DIDN'T KNOW IF I'D SLEPT THE NIGHT OR THE NEXT DAY TOO OR HAD SIMPLY HAD A NAP.

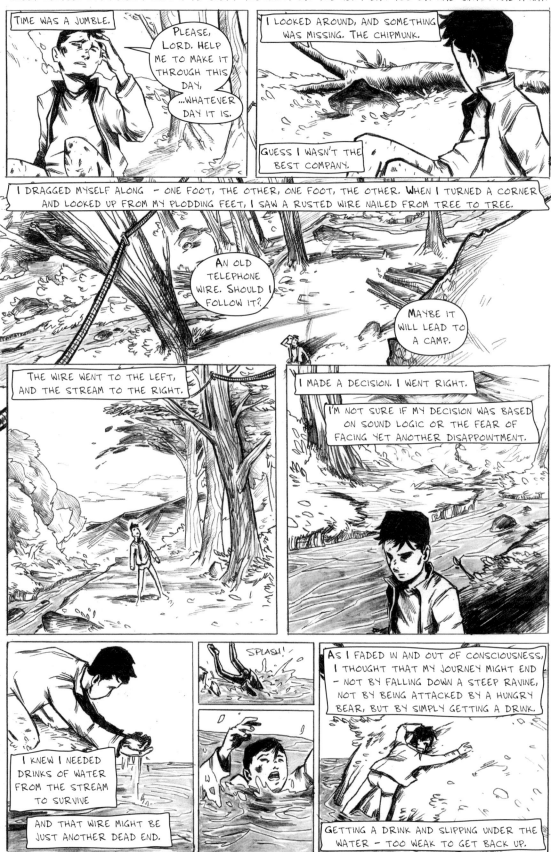

TIME WAS A JUMBLE.

PLEASE, LORD. HELP ME TO MAKE IT THROUGH THIS DAY, ...WHATEVER DAY IT IS.

I LOOKED AROUND, AND SOMETHING WAS MISSING. THE CHIPMUNK.

GUESS I WASN'T THE BEST COMPANY.

I DRAGGED MYSELF ALONG — ONE FOOT, THE OTHER, ONE FOOT, THE OTHER. WHEN I TURNED A CORNER AND LOOKED UP FROM MY PLODDING FEET, I SAW A RUSTED WIRE NAILED FROM TREE TO TREE.

AN OLD TELEPHONE WIRE. SHOULD I FOLLOW IT?

MAYBE IT WILL LEAD TO A CAMP.

THE WIRE WENT TO THE LEFT, AND THE STREAM TO THE RIGHT.

I MADE A DECISION. I WENT RIGHT.

I'M NOT SURE IF MY DECISION WAS BASED ON SOUND LOGIC OR THE FEAR OF FACING YET ANOTHER DISAPPOINTMENT.

I KNEW I NEEDED DRINKS OF WATER FROM THE STREAM TO SURVIVE

AND THAT WIRE MIGHT BE JUST ANOTHER DEAD END.

SPLASH!

AS I FADED IN AND OUT OF CONSCIOUSNESS, I THOUGHT THAT MY JOURNEY MIGHT END — NOT BY FALLING DOWN A STEEP RAVINE, NOT BY BEING ATTACKED BY A HUNGRY BEAR, BUT BY SIMPLY GETTING A DRINK.

GETTING A DRINK AND SLIPPING UNDER THE WATER — TOO WEAK TO GET BACK UP.

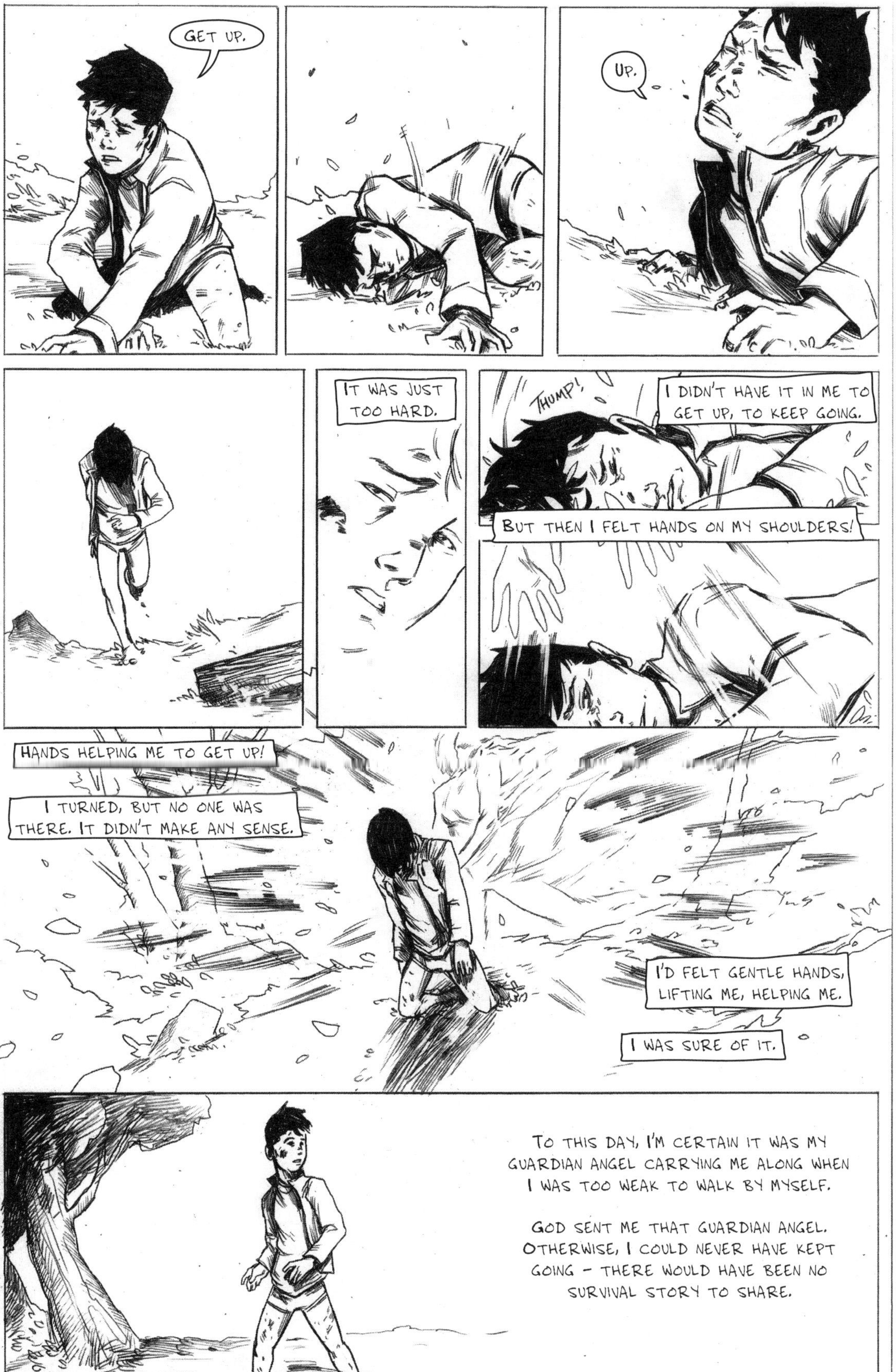
GET UP.
UP.
IT WAS JUST TOO HARD.
THUMP!
I DIDN'T HAVE IT IN ME TO GET UP, TO KEEP GOING.
BUT THEN I FELT HANDS ON MY SHOULDERS!
HANDS HELPING ME TO GET UP!
I TURNED, BUT NO ONE WAS THERE. IT DIDN'T MAKE ANY SENSE.
I'D FELT GENTLE HANDS, LIFTING ME, HELPING ME.
I WAS SURE OF IT.
TO THIS DAY, I'M CERTAIN IT WAS MY GUARDIAN ANGEL CARRYING ME ALONG WHEN I WAS TOO WEAK TO WALK BY MYSELF.
GOD SENT ME THAT GUARDIAN ANGEL. OTHERWISE, I COULD NEVER HAVE KEPT GOING – THERE WOULD HAVE BEEN NO SURVIVAL STORY TO SHARE.

Bangor Daily N

Monday, July 24, 1939

SEARCHERS REFUSE TO RETREAT

Millinocket (AP) - More than 400 searchers continued looking for missing 12-year-old Donn Fendler over the weekend. Monday makes one week since the New York boy disappeared on the top of Mount Katahdin.

Most officials agreed that hopes for finding the boy alive were practically nonexistent. Young Fendler was lost on July 17 during a hike with family and friends. He had no food and was wearing lightweight clothing, not suitable for the severe weather and low nighttime temperatures on the mile-high mountain.

Governor Barrows sent an order for the National Guardsmen to pack up and return home. But forest rangers and volunteers pledged to continue the search to its conclusion. Word went out for searchers to watch for increased sightings of crows, as they likely would lead searchers to the boy's body.

THE NEXT DAY WAS A BLUR. TIME HAD NO MEANING. IT WAS AS IF I WAS WATCHING MY LIFE UNFOLD FROM A DISTANCE...

WHEN I GOT A DRINK IN THE STREAM, I CAME OUT COVERED WITH BLOODSUCKERS. I SCRUBBED THEM OFF WITH SAND.

THEN I FOUND A GUNNYSACK NAILED TO A TREE, I PULLED IT OVER MY HEAD TO KEEP THE BUGS OFF.

BUT THEN I COULDN'T SEE AND TRIPPED OVER A TREE ROOT, TAKING A HUGE CHUNK OUT OF MY TOE.

I SAW BLOOD SPURTING, BUT IT DIDN'T MATTER – I COULDN'T FEEL MY TOE.

I CAME UPON TWO MORE CABINS. I KNEW THEY WERE EMPTY. **ALWAYS** EMPTY.

I SAW A BOG FILLED WITH DEAD TREES THAT LOOKED LIKE DEAD SOLDIERS.

I TURNED AWAY FROM THEIR DEATH STARE.

I SHUFFLED ALONG UNTIL I CRUMPLED FACE DOWN ONTO THE GROUND. I WILLED MYSELF TO GET BACK UP.

BUT I COULDN'T.

Bangor Daily News

Tuesday, July 25, 1939

BOY'S BODY LIKELY FOUND

Millinocket (AP) - On Monday, a search party discovered a foul odor emanating from a deep crevice near the spot where 12-year-old Donn Fendler disappeared on Mount Katahdin. The search party included 16-year-old Henry Condon of Newport, a friend of the young Fendler who was climbing with the boy when they were separated during a storm on the mountain.

Searchers asked Condon to re-enact exactly what happened when Donn Fendler disappeared. Not far from the point of separation, searchers came upon a strong decaying odor arising from a crevice. The crevice was so deep that searchers were unable to see the bottom of it even when they lowered Henry Condon by his ankles headfirst down the crevice as far as possible. Without ropes to lower themselves farther and with darkness approaching, the search team resigned themselves to continuing a search of the crevice on Tuesday.

With the official search over, only about fifty volunteers remained on the mountain, down from 400 searchers at its peak. Employees of Great Northern Paper Company had to return to work on Monday. Even Mr. Donald Fendler, the boy's father, was no longer able to search. On Monday he was admitted to Eastern Maine General Hospital in Bangor with an eye injury he sustained while searching for his son, when a tree branch snapped back and struck him in the eye.

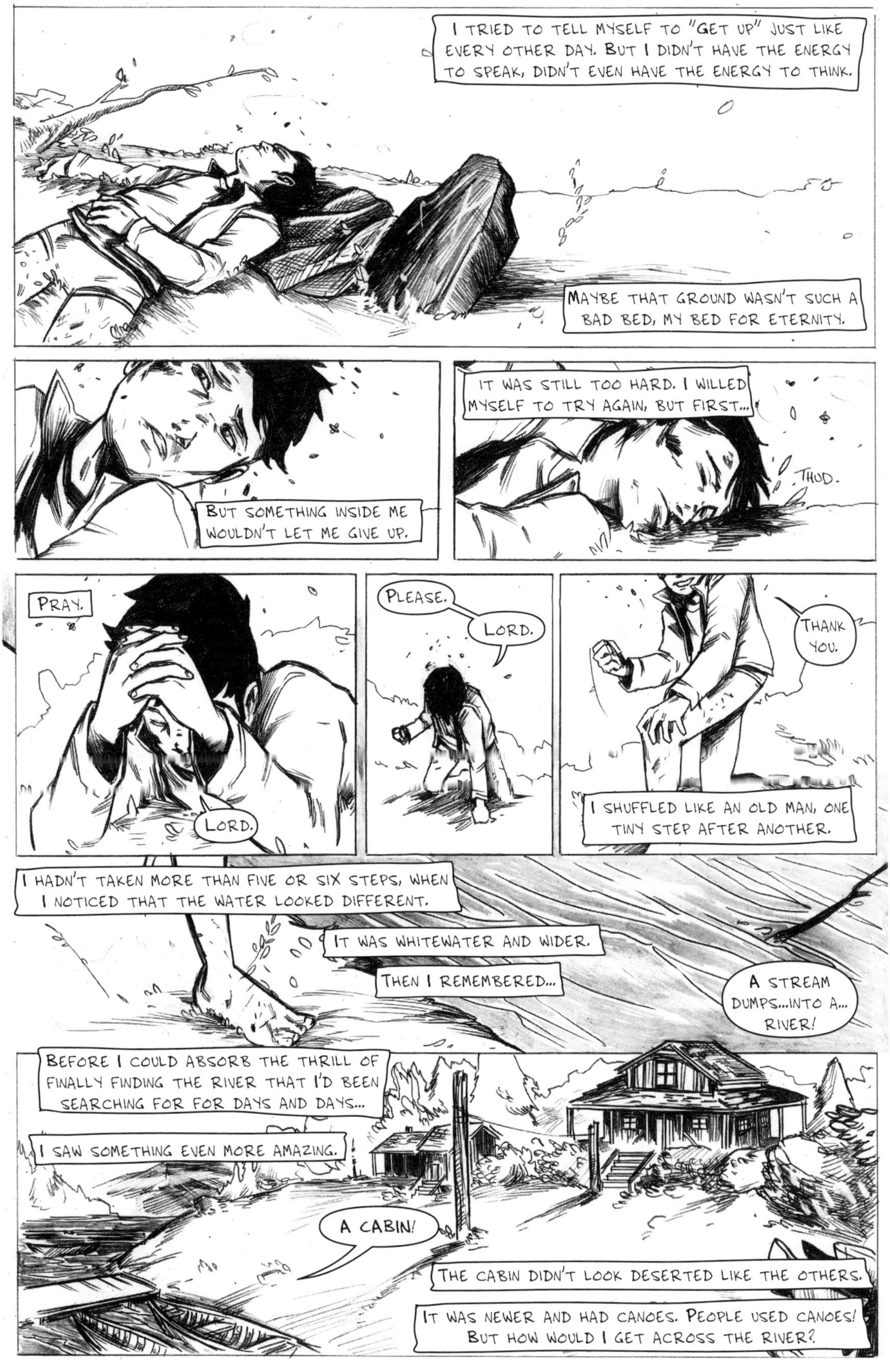
I TRIED TO TELL MYSELF TO "GET UP" JUST LIKE EVERY OTHER DAY. BUT I DIDN'T HAVE THE ENERGY TO SPEAK, DIDN'T EVEN HAVE THE ENERGY TO THINK.
MAYBE THAT GROUND WASN'T SUCH A BAD BED, MY BED FOR ETERNITY.
BUT SOMETHING INSIDE ME WOULDN'T LET ME GIVE UP.
IT WAS STILL TOO HARD. I WILLED MYSELF TO TRY AGAIN, BUT FIRST...
THUD.
PRAY.
LORD.
PLEASE.
LORD.
THANK YOU.
I SHUFFLED LIKE AN OLD MAN, ONE TINY STEP AFTER ANOTHER.
I HADN'T TAKEN MORE THAN FIVE OR SIX STEPS, WHEN I NOTICED THAT THE WATER LOOKED DIFFERENT.
IT WAS WHITEWATER AND WIDER.
THEN I REMEMBERED...
A STREAM DUMPS...INTO A... RIVER!
BEFORE I COULD ABSORB THE THRILL OF FINALLY FINDING THE RIVER THAT I'D BEEN SEARCHING FOR FOR DAYS AND DAYS...
I SAW SOMETHING EVEN MORE AMAZING.
A CABIN!
THE CABIN DIDN'T LOOK DESERTED LIKE THE OTHERS.
IT WAS NEWER AND HAD CANOES. PEOPLE USED CANOES! BUT HOW WOULD I GET ACROSS THE RIVER?

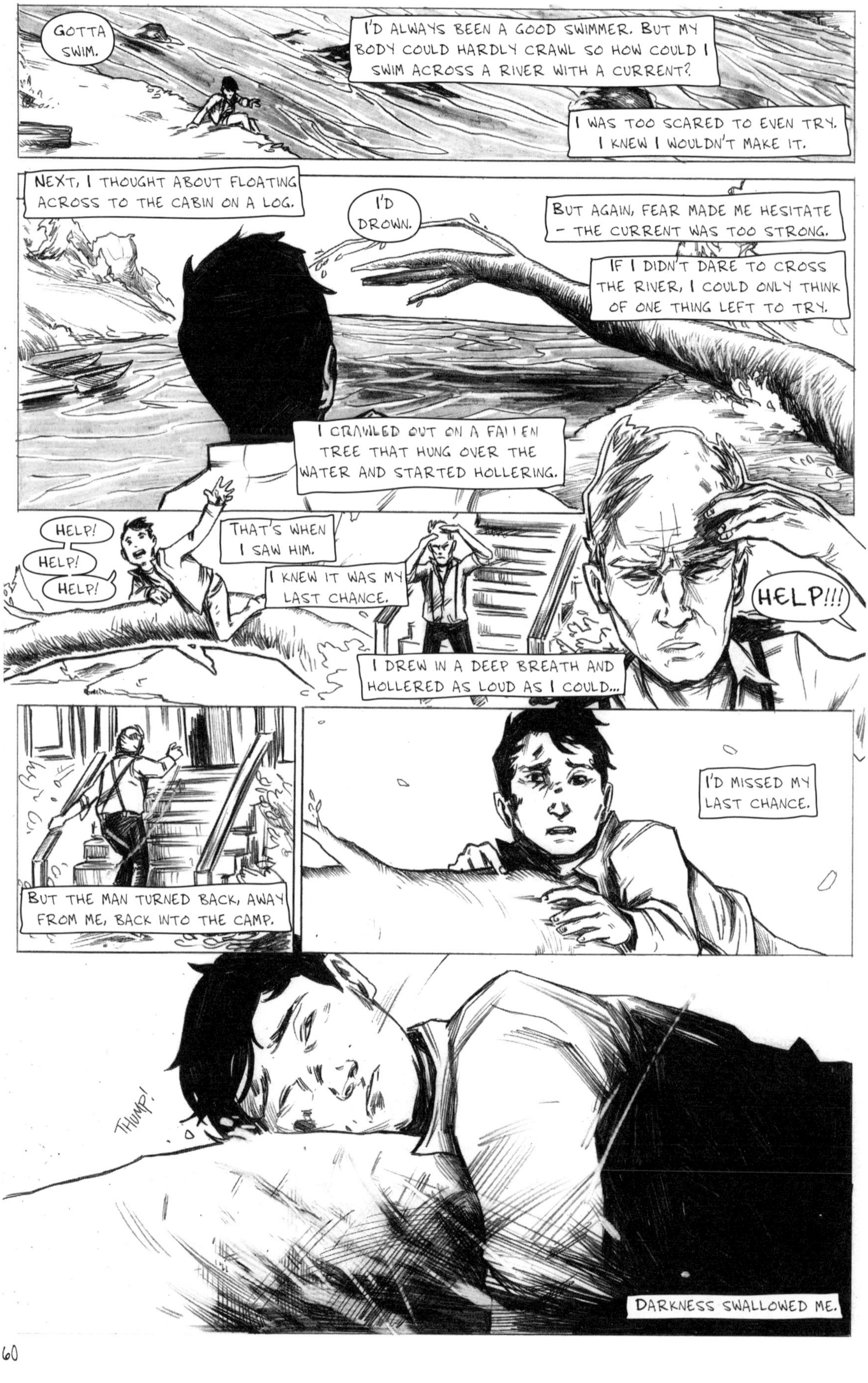
GOTTA SWIM.
I'D ALWAYS BEEN A GOOD SWIMMER. BUT MY BODY COULD HARDLY CRAWL SO HOW COULD I SWIM ACROSS A RIVER WITH A CURRENT?
I WAS TOO SCARED TO EVEN TRY. I KNEW I WOULDN'T MAKE IT.
NEXT, I THOUGHT ABOUT FLOATING ACROSS TO THE CABIN ON A LOG.
I'D DROWN.
BUT AGAIN, FEAR MADE ME HESITATE - THE CURRENT WAS TOO STRONG.
IF I DIDN'T DARE TO CROSS THE RIVER, I COULD ONLY THINK OF ONE THING LEFT TO TRY.
I CRAWLED OUT ON A FALLEN TREE THAT HUNG OVER THE WATER AND STARTED HOLLERING.
HELP!
HELP!
HELP!
THAT'S WHEN I SAW HIM.
I KNEW IT WAS MY LAST CHANCE.
I DREW IN A DEEP BREATH AND HOLLERED AS LOUD AS I COULD...
HELP!!!
BUT THE MAN TURNED BACK, AWAY FROM ME, BACK INTO THE CAMP.
I'D MISSED MY LAST CHANCE.
THUMP!
DARKNESS SWALLOWED ME.

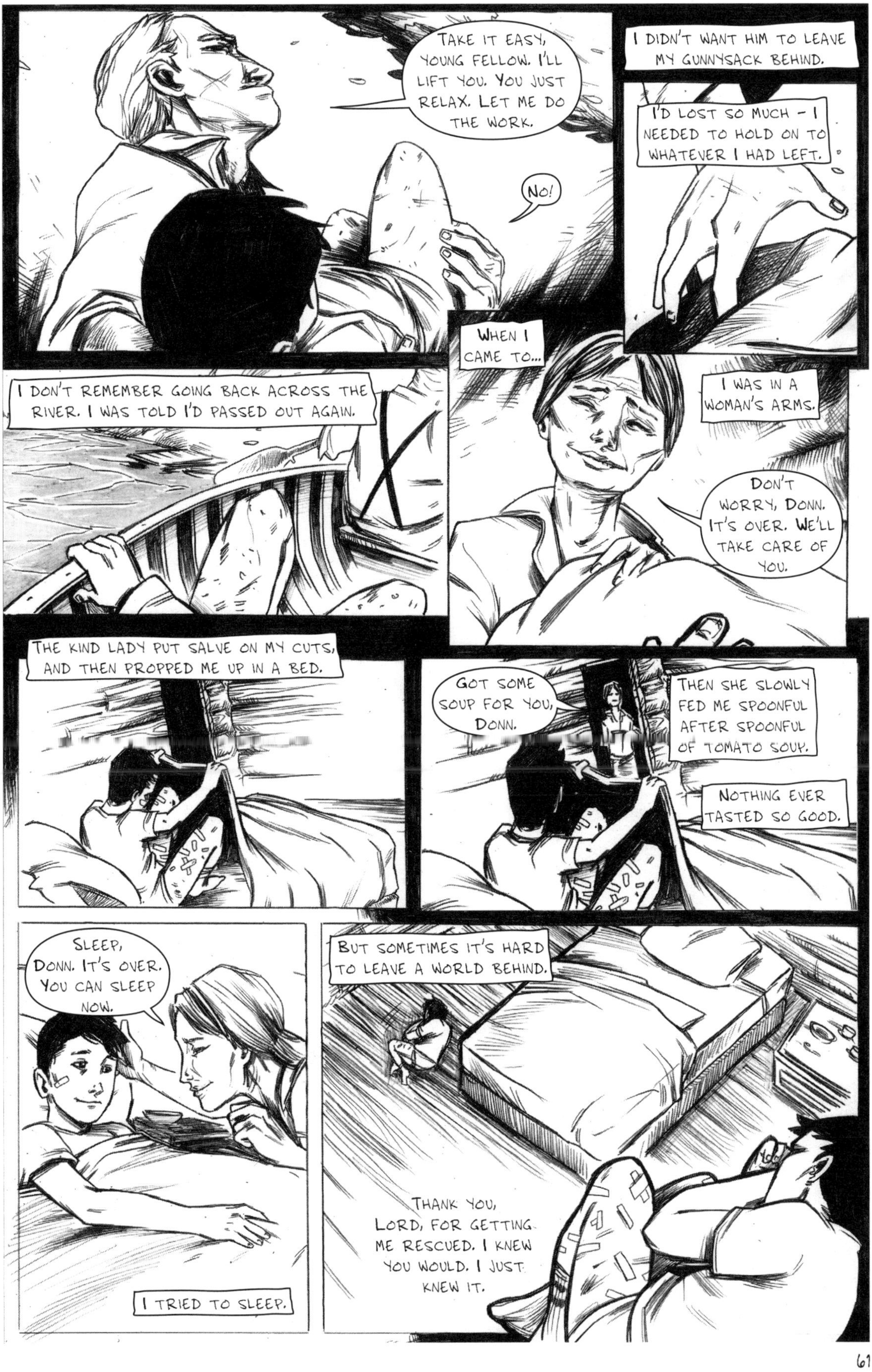
TAKE IT EASY, YOUNG FELLOW. I'LL LIFT YOU. YOU JUST RELAX. LET ME DO THE WORK.
NO!
I DIDN'T WANT HIM TO LEAVE MY GUNNYSACK BEHIND.
I'D LOST SO MUCH – I NEEDED TO HOLD ON TO WHATEVER I HAD LEFT.
I DON'T REMEMBER GOING BACK ACROSS THE RIVER. I WAS TOLD I'D PASSED OUT AGAIN.
WHEN I CAME TO...
I WAS IN A WOMAN'S ARMS.
DON'T WORRY, DONN. IT'S OVER. WE'LL TAKE CARE OF YOU.
THE KIND LADY PUT SALVE ON MY CUTS, AND THEN PROPPED ME UP IN A BED.
GOT SOME SOUP FOR YOU, DONN.
THEN SHE SLOWLY FED ME SPOONFUL AFTER SPOONFUL OF TOMATO SOUP.
NOTHING EVER TASTED SO GOOD.
SLEEP, DONN. IT'S OVER. YOU CAN SLEEP NOW.
I TRIED TO SLEEP.
BUT SOMETIMES IT'S HARD TO LEAVE A WORLD BEHIND.
THANK YOU, LORD, FOR GETTING ME RESCUED. I KNEW YOU WOULD. I JUST KNEW IT.

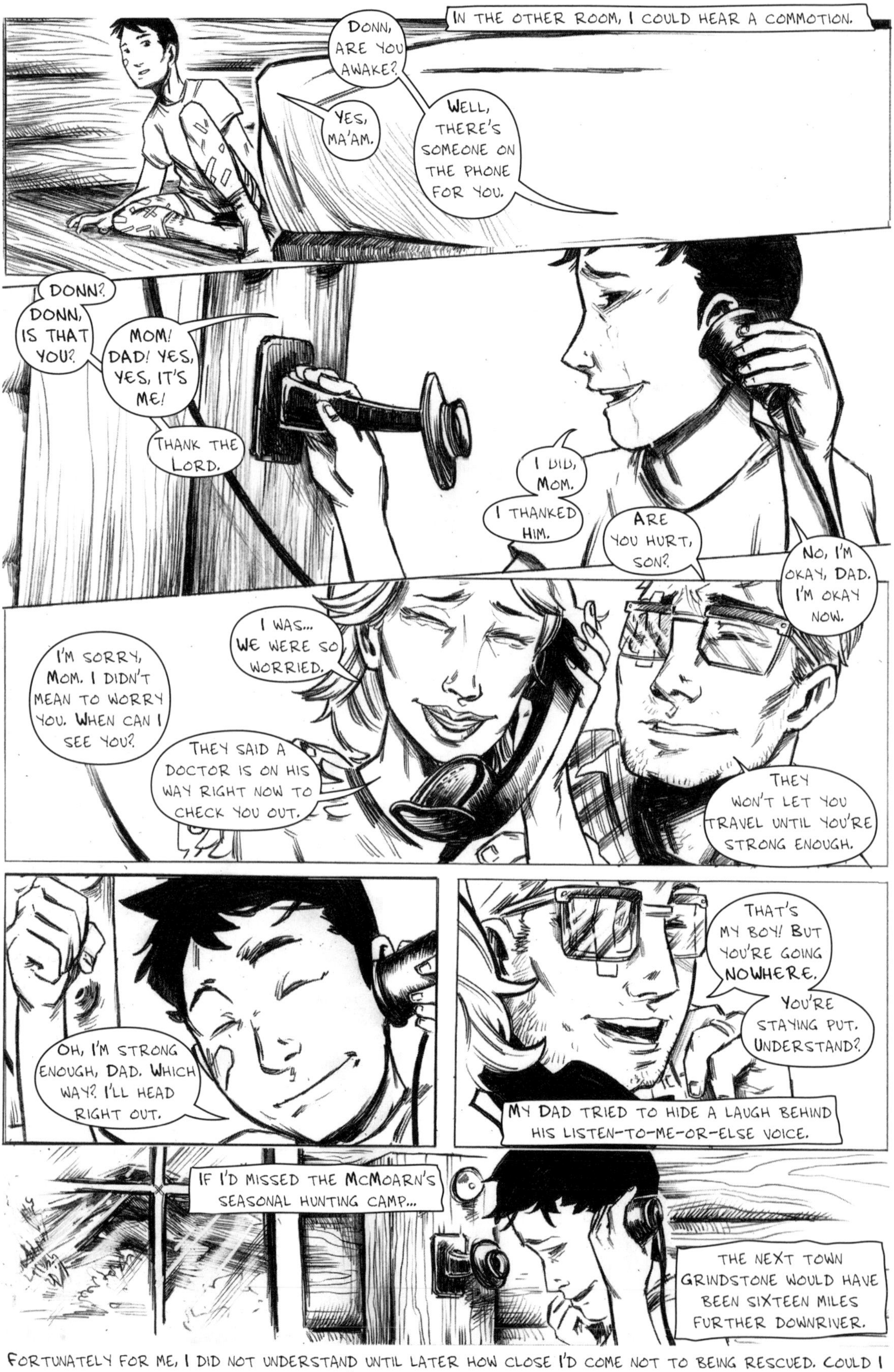

IN THE OTHER ROOM, I COULD HEAR A COMMOTION.
DONN, ARE YOU AWAKE?
YES, MA'AM.
WELL, THERE'S SOMEONE ON THE PHONE FOR YOU.
DONN?
DONN, IS THAT YOU?
MOM! DAD! YES, YES, IT'S ME!
THANK THE LORD.
I DID, MOM.
I THANKED HIM.
ARE YOU HURT, SON?
NO, I'M OKAY, DAD. I'M OKAY NOW.
I WAS... WE WERE SO WORRIED.
I'M SORRY, MOM. I DIDN'T MEAN TO WORRY YOU. WHEN CAN I SEE YOU?
THEY SAID A DOCTOR IS ON HIS WAY RIGHT NOW TO CHECK YOU OUT.
THEY WON'T LET YOU TRAVEL UNTIL YOU'RE STRONG ENOUGH.
OH, I'M STRONG ENOUGH, DAD. WHICH WAY? I'LL HEAD RIGHT OUT.
THAT'S MY BOY! BUT YOU'RE GOING NOWHERE.
YOU'RE STAYING PUT. UNDERSTAND?
MY DAD TRIED TO HIDE A LAUGH BEHIND HIS LISTEN-TO-ME-OR-ELSE VOICE.
IF I'D MISSED THE MCMOARN'S SEASONAL HUNTING CAMP...
THE NEXT TOWN GRINDSTONE WOULD HAVE BEEN SIXTEEN MILES FURTHER DOWNRIVER.

FORTUNATELY FOR ME, I DID NOT UNDERSTAND UNTIL LATER HOW CLOSE I'D COME NOT TO BEING RESCUED. COULD I HAVE MADE IT ANOTHER SIXTEEN MILES? I'M GLAD I NEVER HAD TO LEARN THE ANSWER TO THAT QUESTION.

Later, Mrs. McMoarn brought in Dr. Young and he checked me all over and bandaged my cuts.

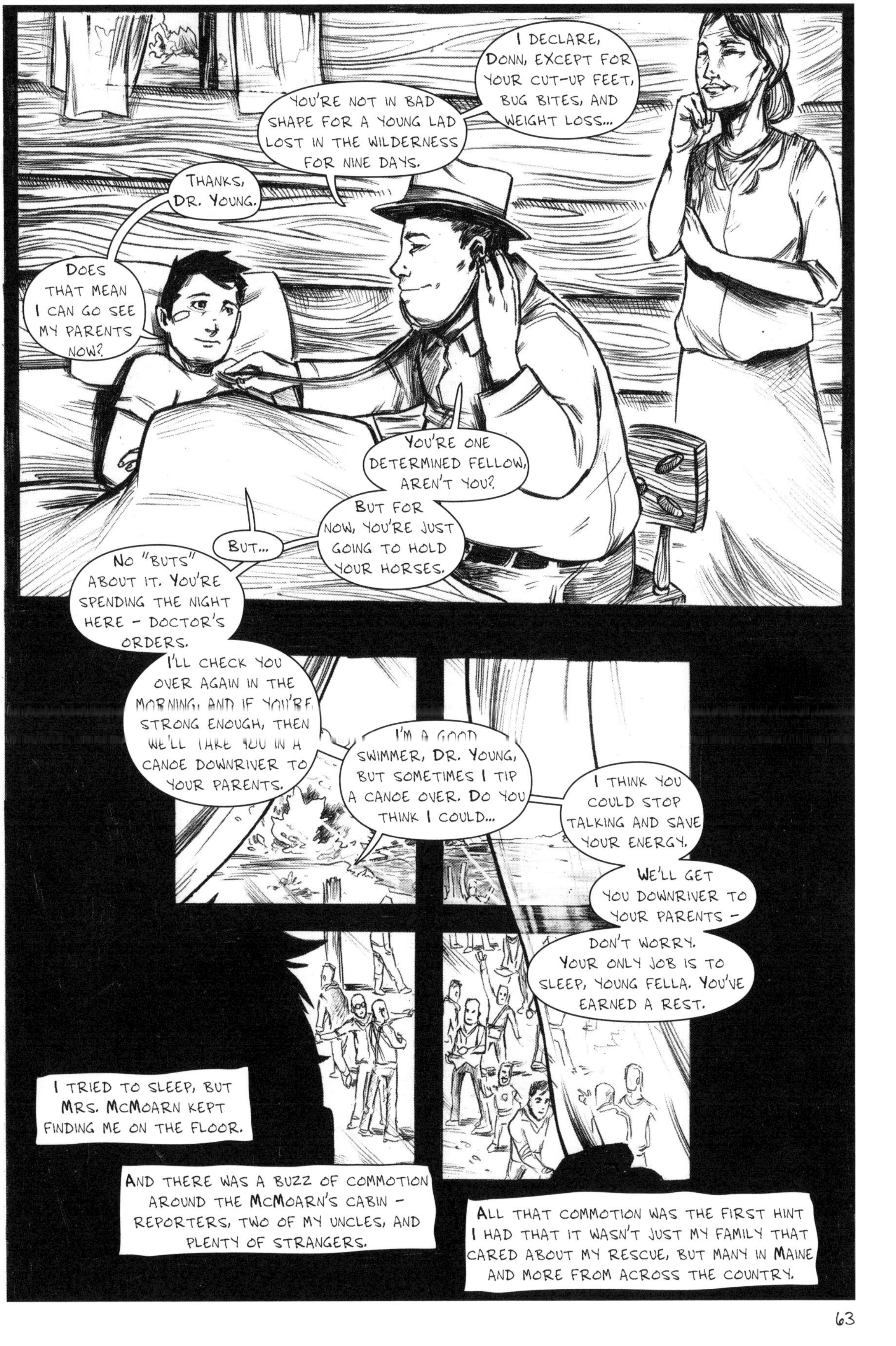
I declare, Donn, except for your cut-up feet, bug bites, and weight loss...
You're not in bad shape for a young lad lost in the wilderness for nine days.
Thanks, Dr. Young.
Does that mean I can go see my parents now?
You're one determined fellow, aren't you?
But for now, you're just going to hold your horses.
But...
No "buts" about it. You're spending the night here – doctor's orders.
I'll check you over again in the morning, and if you're strong enough, then we'll take you in a canoe downriver to your parents.
I'm a good swimmer, Dr. Young, but sometimes I tip a canoe over. Do you think I could...
I think you could stop talking and save your energy.
We'll get you downriver to your parents –
don't worry. Your only job is to sleep, young fella. You've earned a rest.
I tried to sleep, but Mrs. McMoarn kept finding me on the floor.
And there was a buzz of commotion around the McMoarn's cabin – reporters, two of my uncles, and plenty of strangers.
All that commotion was the first hint I had that it wasn't just my family that cared about my rescue, but many in Maine and more from across the country.

DAY TEN

The Bangor Daily New

Wednesday, July 26, 1939

FENDLER BOY FOUND ALIVE!

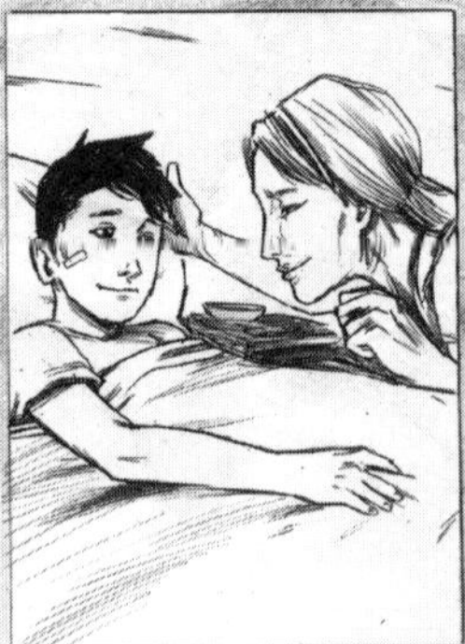

Millinocket (AP) - Against all odds, in what many may call a Maine miracle, 12-year-old Donn Fendler was discovered alive by the owners of Camp Lunksoos on the East Branch of the Penobscot River near Stacyville, more than 35 miles from the spot where the boy was last seen atop Mount Katahdin over a week ago. Searchers expecting to retrieve the boy's body from the mountaintop on Tuesday were incredulous to be called back from the search as word spread that the boy had been found alive so many miles away.

The boy's parents, Mr. and Mrs. Donald Fendler, received the news at Eastern Maine General Hospital in Bangor where Mrs. Fendler was visiting her husband who was injured during the search for their son. After a joyous phone call between son and parents, Mr. and Mrs. Fendler demanded to see their son immediately. Mr. Fendler was not medically cleared to travel. Mrs. Fendler, however, was whisked away by a Maine State Police escort to begin the trip into the North Woods. Before leaving, Mrs. Fendler declared herself "to be the happiest mother in the world. Thank God he's alive and thanks to everyone for the power of their prayers."

One of the Camp Lunksoos owners, Mrs. McMoarn, reported that Donn Fendler told her, "If I'd lain down just once again, I think it would have been the last time. I never could have got back on my feet."

THE NEXT DAY DOCTOR YOUNG CHECKED ME OVER ONE MORE TIME. THEN MRS. MCMOARN PREPARED ME FOR THE CANOE TRIP. SHE GAVE ME A PAIR OF SOCKS AND A PAIR OF PANTS, WHICH SHE'D CUT TO MAKE SMALL ENOUGH TO FIT ME. I ALSO WORE THE SHIRT I'D COME OUT OF THE WOODS WITH AND I CARRIED MY REEFER AND GUNNYSACK.

WHEN IT WAS TIME TO SAY GOODBYE, MRS. MCMOARN SIMPLY NODDED. HER LIPS QUIVERED AS MUCH AS MINE DID.

THANK YOU, MRS. MCMOARN. I'LL NEVER FORGET YOU.

AND I NEVER HAVE.

AS MR. MCMOARN AND MY UNCLES CARRIED ME DOWN TO THE RIVER, I COULD ONLY THINK OF ONE THING... MY FAMILY.

DR. YOUNG, MR. MCMOARN, AND ONE OF MY UNCLES CLIMBED INTO THE CANOE WITH ME AND WE SET OFF.

THE CANOE HAD A SMALL MOTOR THAT PUTT-PUTT-PUTTED US DOWNRIVER.

WHEN WE REACHED SOME RAPIDS, MR. MCMOARN TURNED OFF THE MOTOR AND PADDLED US SAFELY THROUGH TO SMOOTHER WATERS.

AS WE TRAVELED FARTHER AND FARTHER DOWNRIVER, MY STOMACH GOT ALL TINGLY. BUT NOT FROM THE RAPIDS.

HOW MUCH LONGER?

CAN'T BE SURE, DONN. YOUR MOM IS ON HER WAY UPRIVER IN A CANOE TO MEET US. SHOULD BE SOON.

SOON IS AN ETERNITY TO A KID WAITING.

THERE SHE IS!

I SAT UP. I DIDN'T CARE IF THE CANOE ROLLED.

DONN! DONN, IS THAT YOU? ARE YOU ALL RIGHT?

MOM! YES, IT'S ME! I'M GREAT NOW THAT YOU'RE HERE!

THE CANOES CAME TOGETHER — BOTH ALMOST TIPPING OVER — BUT A HUG WAS THE ONLY THING THAT MATTERED.

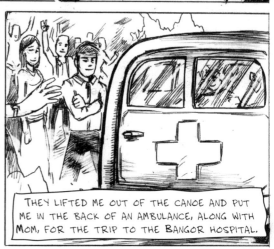

DAD? IS DAD ON HIS WAY, TOO?

YOU'LL SEE HIM SOON. JUST REST.

THERE WAS A HUGE CROWD OF PEOPLE CHEERING FOR US WHEN WE ARRIVED IN GRINDSTONE.

THEY LIFTED ME OUT OF THE CANOE AND PUT ME IN THE BACK OF AN AMBULANCE, ALONG WITH MOM, FOR THE TRIP TO THE BANGOR HOSPITAL.

IT'S GREAT TO BE BACK.

MY MOTHER SIMPLY NODDED.

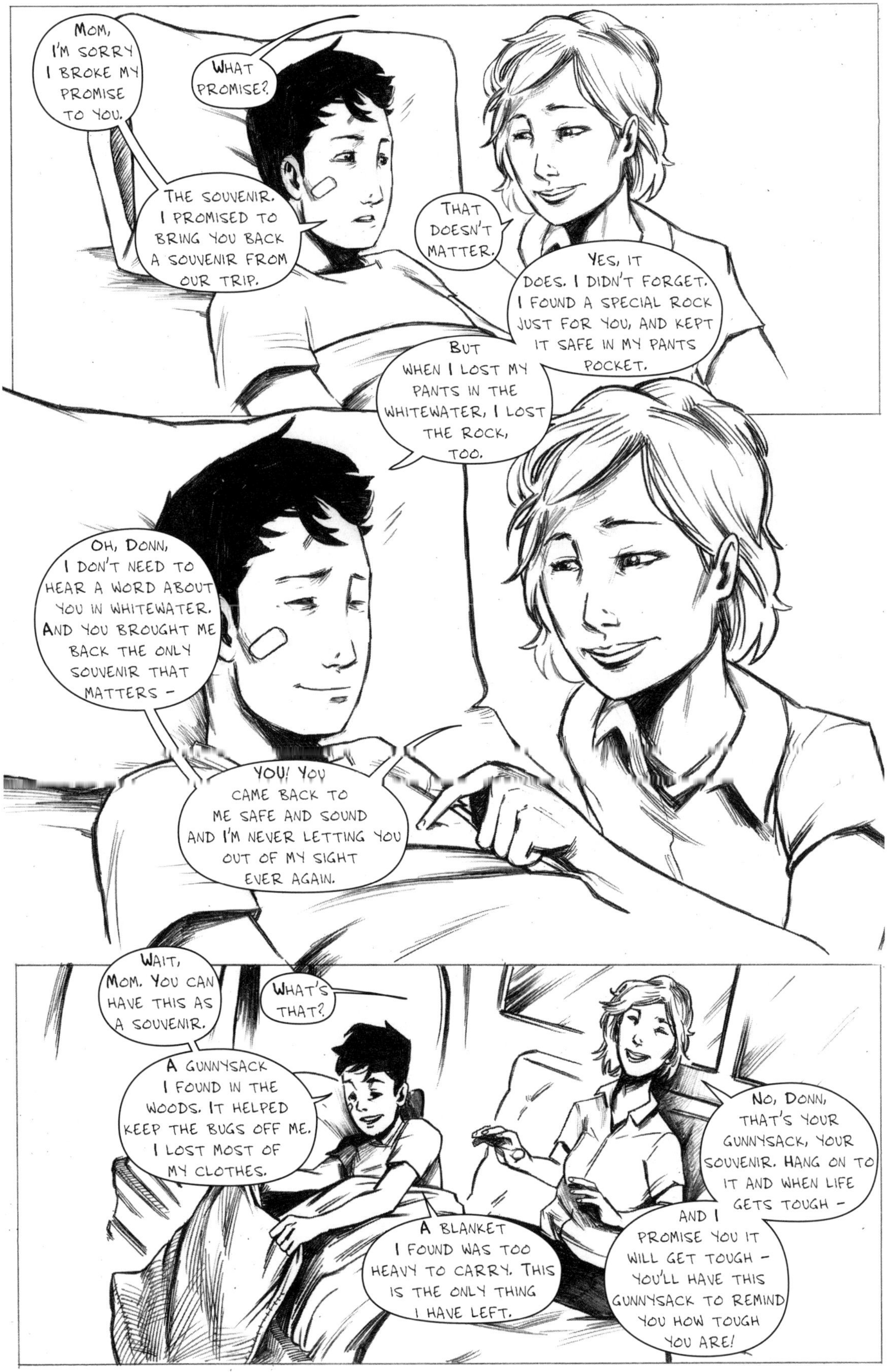
Mom, I'm sorry I broke my promise to you.
What promise?
The souvenir. I promised to bring you back a souvenir from our trip.
That doesn't matter.
Yes, it does. I didn't forget. I found a special rock just for you, and kept it safe in my pants pocket.
But when I lost my pants in the whitewater, I lost the rock, too.
Oh, Donn, I don't need to hear a word about you in whitewater. And you brought me back the only souvenir that matters –
YOU! You came back to me safe and sound and I'm never letting you out of my sight ever again.
Wait, Mom. You can have this as a souvenir.
What's that?
A gunnysack I found in the woods. It helped keep the bugs off me. I lost most of my clothes.
A blanket I found was too heavy to carry. This is the only thing I have left.
No, Donn, that's your gunnysack, your souvenir. Hang on to it and when life gets tough –
And I promise you it will get tough – you'll have this gunnysack to remind you how tough you are!

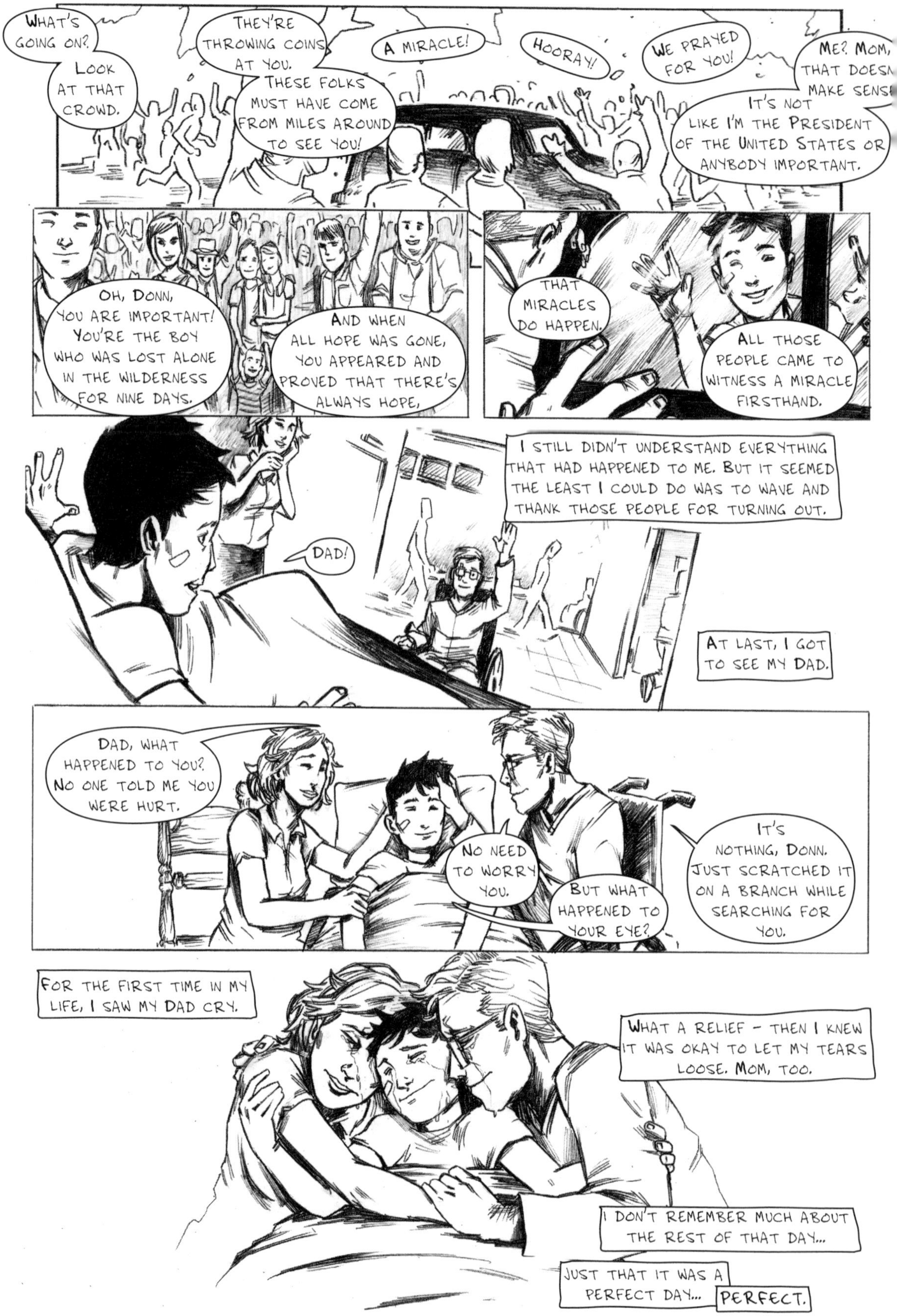
WHAT'S GOING ON?
LOOK AT THAT CROWD.
THEY'RE THROWING COINS AT YOU.
THESE FOLKS MUST HAVE COME FROM MILES AROUND TO SEE YOU!
A MIRACLE!
HOORAY!
WE PRAYED FOR YOU!
ME? MOM, THAT DOESN'T MAKE SENSE.
IT'S NOT LIKE I'M THE PRESIDENT OF THE UNITED STATES OR ANYBODY IMPORTANT.
OH, DONN, YOU ARE IMPORTANT! YOU'RE THE BOY WHO WAS LOST ALONE IN THE WILDERNESS FOR NINE DAYS.
AND WHEN ALL HOPE WAS GONE, YOU APPEARED AND PROVED THAT THERE'S ALWAYS HOPE,
THAT MIRACLES DO HAPPEN.
ALL THOSE PEOPLE CAME TO WITNESS A MIRACLE FIRSTHAND.
I STILL DIDN'T UNDERSTAND EVERYTHING THAT HAD HAPPENED TO ME. BUT IT SEEMED THE LEAST I COULD DO WAS TO WAVE AND THANK THOSE PEOPLE FOR TURNING OUT.
DAD!
AT LAST, I GOT TO SEE MY DAD.
DAD, WHAT HAPPENED TO YOU? NO ONE TOLD ME YOU WERE HURT.
NO NEED TO WORRY YOU.
BUT WHAT HAPPENED TO YOUR EYE?
IT'S NOTHING, DONN. JUST SCRATCHED IT ON A BRANCH WHILE SEARCHING FOR YOU.
FOR THE FIRST TIME IN MY LIFE, I SAW MY DAD CRY.
WHAT A RELIEF - THEN I KNEW IT WAS OKAY TO LET MY TEARS LOOSE. MOM, TOO.
I DON'T REMEMBER MUCH ABOUT THE REST OF THAT DAY...
JUST THAT IT WAS A PERFECT DAY... PERFECT.

Little did I realize this end to my adventure was only the beginning . . .

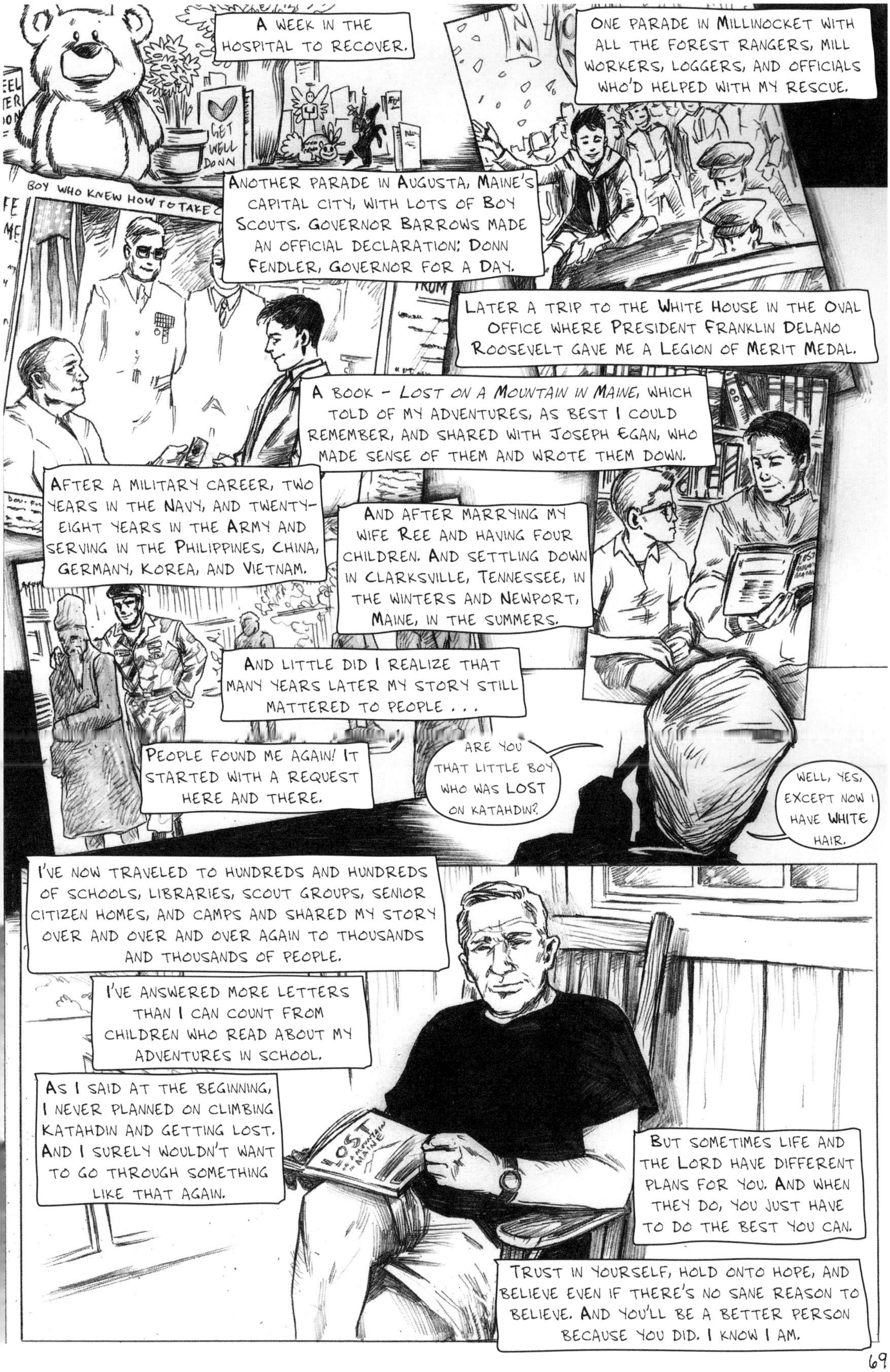

A week in the hospital to recover.
One parade in Millinocket with all the forest rangers, mill workers, loggers, and officials who'd helped with my rescue.
Another parade in Augusta, Maine's capital city, with lots of Boy Scouts. Governor Barrows made an official declaration: Donn Fendler, Governor for a Day.
Later a trip to the White House in the Oval Office where President Franklin Delano Roosevelt gave me a Legion of Merit Medal.
A book – Lost on a Mountain in Maine, which told of my adventures, as best I could remember, and shared with Joseph Egan, who made sense of them and wrote them down.
After a military career, two years in the Navy, and twenty-eight years in the Army and serving in the Philippines, China, Germany, Korea, and Vietnam.
And after marrying my wife Ree and having four children. And settling down in Clarksville, Tennessee, in the winters and Newport, Maine, in the summers.
And little did I realize that many years later my story still mattered to people . . .
People found me again! It started with a request here and there.
Are you that little boy who was lost on Katahdin?
Well, yes, except now I have white hair.
I've now traveled to hundreds and hundreds of schools, libraries, scout groups, senior citizen homes, and camps and shared my story over and over and over again to thousands and thousands of people.
I've answered more letters than I can count from children who read about my adventures in school.
As I said at the beginning, I never planned on climbing Katahdin and getting lost. And I surely wouldn't want to go through something like that again.
But sometimes life and the Lord have different plans for you. And when they do, you just have to do the best you can.
Trust in yourself, hold onto hope, and believe even if there's no sane reason to believe. And you'll be a better person because you did. I know I am.

Some of the Questions I've Been Asked Most Often Through the Years

A Q&A with Donn Fendler

Q-Did you ever go back to Katahdin?

A-Yes, in 1977, I climbed Katahdin again with some relatives, friends, and reporters. They didn't let me out of their sight for a second. I was older and it was harder for me to climb. I had to stop for frequent rests. Once when I was resting, a young boy and his parents passed me on the trail. I asked the boy if he was going to the top. He replied, "Yes, and I'm going to meet Donn Fendler up there." I said, "Well, actually, you're meeting him right here." He didn't believe me and raced ahead. I've been to the base of Katahdin many other times to give talks. Each time I return, the rangers tease me that as soon as I arrive in Baxter State Park they get on their two-way radios and spread the word: "He's baaaaaaaack. Keep your eyes out. Don't let him get lost . . . again!"

Q-What was your secret to surviving all those days out in the wilderness?

A-I believe I owe my survival to three things: (1) My faith in God and prayers—

not only did I pray while I was lost, but people from across Maine and the country prayed for me to get out safely. (2) My Boy Scout training that taught me to stay calm and to follow a stream. (3) My will to live—I wouldn't give up even when all seemed hopeless.

Q-What did you eat while you were lost?

A-Fortunately, I had never been a big eater, so I didn't crave food as much as you might think. The water, which was always nearby in the stream, kept me going. I saw chokeberries, but I didn't dare to eat them because I'd heard they could make me sick. I ate strawberries, but probably no more than a half a cup over all those days.

Q-What was the worst part of your experience?

A-The bugs—they were everywhere . . . there wasn't a spot on me that wasn't covered in bug bites. I couldn't escape them no matter how hard I tried.

Q-What did you learn from being lost?

A-Being lost strengthened my faith in God, taught me to be responsible for my actions, and made me realize what love of family is all about, that I would never, ever take my family for granted—even my annoying sisters!

Q-Do you still have that gunnysack?

A-I used to take it with me when I gave talks. But it got so ripped and worn out after being handled by so many people, there was nothing left to it. But I still carry my reefer (jacket) for people to see when I give talks. I also treasure the Legion of Merit Medal I received from President Roosevelt and a 1939 letter I received from Percival Baxter who told me I was "a very brave and plucky boy."

Q-Why do you think people are still so interested in your story after all this time? And why do you keep sharing it?

A-I'm not sure why people are still interested in my adventure more than 70 years after it happened. It amazes me. Maybe as time goes on and there are more high-tech gadgets like cell phones and GPSs, people find what happened to me even harder to believe. Most twelve-year-old kids today probably can't imagine not being "connected" and able to reach anyone, anytime, anywhere. Times were different then. I think some people like to imagine what they would have done if they'd gotten lost. And, gosh, even to this day, I think that maybe I did experience a miracle—to make it out alive. I do know why I keep sharing my story. My adventure is all about faith and determination—something kids in the world today should know more about. As long as people are interested and as long as I'm able to, I'll keep telling my story. It's the least I can do. After all, all those rescuers, the state of Maine, and people from all across the country worked hard and prayed hard for my rescue. It's my small way of giving back.

DONN FENDLER was born in New York City in 1926 and raised in nearby Rye, New York. He joined the navy in World War II as a Sea Bee serving in the Pacific and China. He then graduated from Benedictine College in Atchison, Kansas. Donn returned to serve his country as an Infantry Airborne Officer in the U.S. Army, retiring after thirty years with the rank of lieutenant colonel. He now splits his time between Clarksville, Tennessee, and Newport, Maine. Through the years, he has given countless talks at schools, libraries, and to Scout troops about his survival tale recounted in the 1939 book *Lost on a Mountain in Maine*.

LYNN PLOURDE (www.lynnplourde.com) is the author of more than twenty-five picture books, including *Only Cows Allowed* and *The First Feud*, an original fable about Mount Katahdin. Her books have been included on several "Best Books" lists. Lynn's work on *Lost Trail* with her friend Donn Fendler is her first graphic novel. She lives in Winthrop, Maine.

BEN BISHOP is a graphic novel creator, toy designer, and illustrator from Maine. Ben wrote, illustrated, and self-published his first book, *Nathan the Caveman*, in 2008 followed by several other smaller works. He is currently working on his next graphic novel, *Something Like Falling,* and doing the artwork for the Ardden/Atlas entertainment comic book *The Stand-In*, written by comics legend Jim Krueger. See more of Ben's work at www.bishart.net.